From Playground

to Prostitute

From Playground to Prostitute

Based on a true story of salvation

Elanie Kruger

with Jaco Hough-Coetzee

Foreword by Hykie Berg

DELTA PUBLISHERS

Johannesburg & Cape Town

Originally published in Afrikaans as *Van Skoolbank tot Bordeelbed*

First English edition published in South Africa in 2015 by
DELTA PUBLISHERS, an imprint of
JONATHAN BALL PUBLISHERS
A division of Media24 Limited
PO Box 33977
Jeppestown
2043

ISBN 978-1-92824-801-9
ebook ISBN 978-1-92824-802-6

Every effort has been made to trace the copyright holders and to obtain their permission for the use of copyright material. The publishers apologise for any errors or omissions and would be grateful to be notified of any corrections that should be incorporated in future editions of this book.

Twitter: www.twitter.com/JonathanBallPub
Facebook: www.facebook.com/JonathanBallPublishers
Blog: http://jonathanball.bookslive.co.za/

Cover by Michiel Botha
Translated by Jozua van der Lugt
Design and typesetting by Nazli Jacobs

Printed by *paarlmedia*, a division of Novus Holdings

Set in 10.5 on 16pt Bookman

To all the victims of human trafficking –
there is hope, there is healing and the shackles
will be undone . . . you are not alone.

Foreword

Having heard about Elanie Kruger in 2012, I contacted her and we agreed to meet at a restaurant in Randburg. At the time I was closely involved with PSARU (People Search and Rescue Unit), an organisation that locates and returns missing children and adults, some of them victims of human trafficking. I was curious to hear Elanie's story, and could not believe what I heard as it unfolded. The picture she painted didn't agree with the gentle figure sitting opposite me. Her story would make anyone's hair stand on end, and this nightmare of an experience would be seared into her memory, I soon realised. It is amazing that she survived it all.

Later, I would get to know another side to her: her burning passion not only to help victims of human trafficking but also to be proactive and keep others from falling into the same trap. She is utterly committed to putting a stop to this evil.

We became friends, and together gave numerous talks at various venues across the country to create an awareness of human trafficking. She tells her story honestly and with an open mind, something few people will be prepared for. Today

Elanie Kruger isn't scared any more: she is fearless and unwavering in the task she has set herself.

She also means a lot to PSARU – something the team and I are very grateful for.

People might get the impression that she is tough and thick-skinned, yet she's just like any other girl – somebody with a heart filled with dreams. A girl is still a girl.

Elanie's story is told in riveting fashion by Jaco Hough-Coetzee. The story of a brave and fearless woman whose undaunted obedience to God, combined with an unselfish service to the community, is the driving force that helps her make a difference in the lives of the victims of this heinous crime.

Hykie Berg
www.hykieberg.com

Part one
Into darkness

One

The peak-hour traffic exiting the city centre cruises slowly from traffic light to traffic light. It's raining softly. Pieter and Engela are driving in the opposite direction down Church Street, from Oranjesig towards town.

'It's Friday, 15 October 1993, and the weekend has arrived!' chatters Jaco de Wet on the car radio. 'The weather service predicts a gloomy and wet weekend for Bloemfontein, but the sounds of Radio Oranje will keep things cosy. So, let's get going with Billy Joel's latest hit single, "The River of Dreams".'

Engela hums along to the song. She is in a happy mood because she's on her way to her first job. Every now and then, Pieter's eyes wander over the sixteen-year-old passenger next to him. She's bloody attractive, he thinks. She's wearing tight jeans that accentuate her long legs. The curves under her red blouse confirm her transition from teenager to young woman. Engela looks at him and smiles. He smiles rigidly, quickly shifts his eyes back to the road and changes to third gear. Inside him two voices are arguing: No, Pieter, it's wrong what you're doing, says one. She's a human being. To hell with that, the second voice invades his thoughts. She has done it, after all. Her brother told him. She knows all too well how to do it. Again, the first voice: No, Pieter. No! Pieter suddenly hesitates. He slows the vehicle down and steers into the left lane. Do you have a choice, Pieter? Another solution? No, Pieter, you don't. Do it and be done!

'What's wrong?' Engela wants to know.

'Nothing. Just careful because of the rain.'

* * *

Six months ago Pieter discovered, through a classified advertisement in *Volksblad*, the Lady Femmé club in Bloemfontein's city centre, on the corner of Oos Burger and Charles streets. The entrance fee was steep, a full R100, but so what, he thought. It was his twenty-fourth birthday; he was alone and didn't want to be. Why not splash out a little? It's only once a year, he convinced himself. That evening Pieter found himself sitting at the bar counter, sipping on a brandy and Coke, and staring at the enticing goods delightfully on display under the girls' tight, skimpy garments. A girl with big blue eyes sat down next to him. Jacky, she introduced herself and crossed her legs in his direction.

He offers a hand. 'Pieter. Pleased to meet you.'

'First time, right? I always remember a handsome face when I see one,' she says and caresses his cheek. Jacky is a few years older than him.

Pieter feels the excitement stirring between his legs – no one has ever called him handsome. 'Well, yes. My first time. I am kind of busy with my . . . my business ventures,' he apologises half-heartedly. 'Can hardly find the time to go out.'

'Really?' she asks playfully. 'So, if I may ask, Pete, what do you do that keeps you so busy?'

Pieter takes two quick gulps from his brandy and Coke. Now you have to think carefully, Pieter, flashes through his brain. Now you have to think very carefully! Admitting you're a mechanic won't cut it in this place. He glances at the other men; they all seem to be high-profile guys. Some in suits, others in expensive designer clothes. Pieter is relieved he's wearing his best outfit for a night on the town, yet his denims and T-shirt are no match.

'Imports,' he says, unnecessarily loudly. 'Anything. Especially from Europe.' He doesn't notice the guy behind the bar counter suddenly show an interest in him.

Jacky leans into him, confidingly: 'Then you will feel right at home, Pete. The chaps hanging out here are all successful businessmen. Just like yourself.' Her eyes glide across the room. 'Doctors, attorneys, architects, business owners, city councillors. Those types, you know.'

'Yes, like I said, I am rather busy. In fact, there is this major transaction in China waiting.'

'Then we will have to spend your precious time properly tonight,' Jacky coos in his ear. A breast brushes against his arm. 'Call me over when you're up for a little fun.'

She gets up and walks over to the pool table on the other side of the bar. He orders a fourth drink. Damn, he thinks, I'm in the right place. Guys with big money hang out in this joint. Guys with connections and needs. Guys you have to befriend if you want to do something with your life and start your own business. He decides he has to come back to build up his contacts. After all, it's not who you are, but who you know. The only problem is, on his R1 500 monthly salary from Nick's Auto Repairs he can't exactly afford to hang out with these big shots. A man sits next to him and introduces himself as Steve. 'I believe you're in imports?' Pieter nods.

'Interesting. Like what?'

The four doubles have turned Pieter into a big man by now. A clever man. A man with a vision. Anything, he responds. Dirt cheap and without any annoying paperwork. And of course the Receiver needn't know about any of these transactions, he winks.

Steve observes the man in front of him, in his jeans and white T-shirt. 'But why haven't I heard about you? Bloemfontein is a small town, as you know.'

'Because I work undercover,' Pieter retorts. He's been expecting this one, after all.

'You're not bullshitting me, right?'

Pieter shakes his head, lights a cigarette nonchalantly and takes another sip of his drink. His smile is all confidence. No, not lying, the smile proclaims. Okay, maybe a little, he thinks, but they don't need to know that. His massive import business and all his contracts are still only a dream, but he needs customers to make them a reality. And here they are, sitting right in front of him. The guys with the money.

Steve clinks Pieter's glass. 'We'll chat again – if we see each other again.'

Steve disappears somewhere in the club and Pieter remains at the bar counter, alone. Damn, I was good, he thinks. One of these days he won't be buried in oily engines any more.

'Anthony Grand,' someone suddenly exclaims next to him. 'I am one of the partners. Another?' he asks and points at Pieter's empty glass.

But Pieter's wallet is empty. 'No thanks. Home time.'

'Last one. On the house.'

Pieter nods in agreement. Anthony orders two doubles, one for each of them. 'Cheers.' Anthony clinks Pieter's glass jovially. 'So, I hear you can get anything?'

'Yup.'

'Anything, as in anything?'

'Yup.'

'In that case . . . I think I might have a deal for you. Maybe even two. How big can you go?'

Suddenly Pieter's confidence has no limits. 'How big would you like me to go?'

Anthony bursts into laughter. 'I like what I hear. I like. Cheers.' Their glasses touch a second time in the dimly lit club, ice cubes tinkling.

'Will you be here tomorrow night?' Anthony asks. He gestures to the man behind the counter to pass the Ritmeester cigar box. He opens the lid and holds it out invitingly to Pieter, who immediately takes one. Anthony's golden Zippo lighter flickers in front of Pieter's face.

'Yes,' Pieter replies without a second thought. 'I think so.'

A thick cloud of cigar smoke flutters about the club owner's face. Anthony quietly observes the young man sitting in front of him. 'Fine,' he says. 'Let's make it around ten.'

Pieter realises it was an order. He's back the following evening.

At exactly ten to ten he presses the bell next to the club security gate. The young man at reception activates a buzzer hidden under his desk and the gate clicks open.

'Welcome, Anthony's expecting you,' Jacques says.

Pieter follows him through the bar section and then down a long passage. There are three doors on the left and four on the right. Shrieks of sexual pleasure can be heard coming from two of the rooms. The passage comes to a dead end at a wooden door with a sign affixed to it that reads 'PRIVATE'. Jacques knocks three times before turning the silver knob. They step into a luxurious lounge furnished with black leather couches arranged around a rectangular coffee table. Cigar smoke hangs heavily in the pale light, almost obscuring the huge erotic painting on one wall.

'Pieter! Pieter!' Anthony calls out as he gets up from his chair. He welcomes Pieter with a jovial embrace. 'Sit down. What are you drinking? Cognac?'

Pieter nods in agreement, greets Steve sitting to his left and offers his hand to the stranger on the couch opposite the table. He looks Greek, his long black hair in a ponytail down the back of his neck. The thick gold chain around his neck and the massive ring flashing on his finger stand out against his black trousers and open-neck shirt.

'Mark, Pieter,' Anthony introduces the two as Jacques closes the door behind him, only to reappear moments later with three glasses of Cognac on a silver tray. Doubles, on the rocks. Mark observes Pieter through narrowed eyes and doesn't say much. Anthony paints the background to the transaction matter-of-factly: Mark is shopping for a Porsche 911, new, a 1993 model, but '92 will also do. Delivered in Welkom, under the radar. Private and discreet. New engine number and all the required documents to satisfy the road hawks. And it doesn't matter from where Pieter's connections snatch it. Mark still says nothing, and simply stares at Pieter as he swirls the ice cubes in his glass. Pieter swallows hard. He considers his options. Wouldn't it be sensible to opt out right now? Maybe things were moving just a little too fast after last night's bravado. Maybe he should just get up and say: 'Sorry guys, I can't do it.' And walk away. Mark's and Anthony's eyes are fixed on him. Steve exhales a cloud of smoke. Pieter wonders if they can tell he's bluffing. Mark leans forward and carefully tips his cigar ash into the ashtray on the table between them.

'Your fee . . . is R20 000 for the car,' Mark says as he leans back on the couch.

Gosh, Pieter thinks. That's more than ten months' salary.

'Of course, that excludes your expenses.' Mark crosses his legs. 'How much would that be?'

Pieter is at a loss for words. He has no contacts or experience in the underworld. Frankly, he has no idea where and how to steal a car, or how to falsify the engine number and paperwork and deliver it in Welkom. 'It might take a while. Maybe a month. Maybe two,' Pieter offers, playing for time.

'And your expenses? How much?' Marks asks, again.

'We'll see . . . it depends . . .'

There's a hint of irritation in Mark's voice. He wants to seal the deal. 'Say what, let's make it R50 000. Would that be enough?'

Pieter nods.

'Can't hear you,' Mark says. 'I'm asking: R50 000 for expenses, R20 000 for your fee. Do we have a deal?'

'Yes . . . we have a deal.' Pieter's voice isn't quite as self-assured as he'd hoped.

'Bravo. Bravo.' Mark claps his hands slowly. He reaches into his pocket, produces a fistful of notes and chucks the money on the coffee table. 'That's two thousand. An advance. The rest you'll get on delivery. Agreed?'

Pieter can see no other choice. 'Agreed,' he says and lifts his glass to Mark before gulping down the rest of the Cognac.

'You said two months? Max?' Mark asks.

'Two months. Yes.'

'To a successful meeting, then.' Anthony smiles broadly. Pieter wonders how much he'll be pocketing from this.

'One last thing . . .' Mark's voice has a threatening tone as he stands in front of Pieter. 'Don't screw with me. Don't even try. You won't know what hit you. Understood?'

Then, to Anthony: 'Enough talking for one night. Get me a girl. I want the redhead.'

Two

The first voice still wants to argue: Don't, Pieter! But it's the other one that's winning the debate. Pieter drives faster. They'll be there in ten minutes. He starts in surprise when Engela lays her hand innocently on his thigh.

'Thanks, Pieter,' she says softly. 'You're a pal.'

He quickly turns his head, taking in her happy smile. 'It's nothing,' he says, playing it down. 'That's why we're there for each other.'

'If it wasn't for you . . . thanks . . .' She crosses her arms and stares at the raindrops on the windscreen. The wipers remove them in seconds. Swoosh, swoosh, she mimics the sound softly. The job Pieter has organised for her will wash away the tears in just the same way. The excitement flows through her – finally, a job that will change her life.

'What kind of work is it?' she asks. 'And . . . will they even take me?' She has doubts all of a sudden. Since running away from school three weeks ago and leaving Dewetsdorp behind, she's been looking for a job in Bloemfontein. Unsuccessfully.

Pieter smiles. He stops at the red traffic light at the Selborne

Avenue crossing. 'Of course, they will take you.' Geez, girl, if only you knew how fast they'd take you! The light changes to green. First gear, second gear. Swoosh, swoosh, the wipers sweep the water from the windscreen, but it stays wet. Like when a person cries, Engela thinks. You can wipe the tears from your eyes, but your eyes stay wet. And hasn't she cried more than ever in her life this year? Or maybe not. Maybe every year will have its share of crying, but as soon as the next cry comes along you forget about yesterday's. For as long as she can remember she has cried. When she was a little girl in Brits, before they moved to Bloemfontein, she cried about the poverty, the hunger and the fighting at home. These three things have always been part of her life. Food was often scarce in her house, and the sheriff of the court often paid a visit, because money was rare – thanks to dad Andries' and mum Dorothy's heavy drinking – and then, of course, the arguing after every drinking session. Three years ago her mother moved from their house in Fauna, on the edge of Bloemfontein, to a flat in the centre of the city, and Engela stayed behind with her dad. There was a new man in her mother's life, and after a year – in 1991 – she followed him out to Dewetsdorp. Engela went along, but in Uncle Joshua's house the arguing and drinking were just as bad. Engela cried through it all, until after her mother's funeral in February this year. Her dad and his new wife, Susan, then also moved to Dewetsdorp so that Engela could stay with them and not have to change schools again. At the time they were unaware of what Engela was getting up to behind their backs.

'What kind of work is it? Do you know?' Engela wants to know again as Pieter continues driving in the afternoon rain.

Third gear. 'Nothing difficult. Screw all those other dudes who didn't want to employ you. You'll see.'

Yes, screw them, thinks the girl who should really be in her bedroom in the house in Dewetsdorp, doing her standard eight homework. But she had to escape to Bloemfontein, as Group 13 was after her. She was scared. Very scared. Marius had been sending her messages: 'When we get hold of you, you're dead!'

*   *   *

Sergeant Pieterse would pick her up at home every morning and drive her to school, and would drop her off again at two o'clock every afternoon. But, from a distance, Marius du Preez was keeping an eye on her in the school grounds. This mysterious matric boy, with the hate-filled eyes, was the leader of Group 13, a gang nobody really wanted to tangle with; everyone was scared of them. Only two months ago Engela was still part of the gang.

'It made me feel good,' she explains to Sergeant Pieterse during one of his many interrogations. 'Kind of . . . immortal.'

Wednesday 25 August 1993, Pieterse scribbles at the top of the page in his notebook. 'Immortal?' He lifts his eyebrows as he looks at her. 'How come?'

Engela doesn't respond immediately. It's the same question she's been asking herself over and over. 'I think . . . it seemed no one understood me. At school . . .'

'Yes? At school?' Pieterse encourages her when she stops talking.

'No one wanted to be my friend. Everybody knew about me, where I come from. The poor sod from Bloemfontein whose mum and dad were more often pissed than on their feet. Everyone knew my stepdad as well – the man who would let the liquor flow as easily and then pull out his gun when he couldn't have his way. I felt like an outsider at school, Sergeant. That's the thing. No one really wanted to hang out with me, but I understand why. I don't think I blame them. But Marius was different. He started talking to me. I knew how the others were gossiping about me. The guy has gone mad also, they would joke later. It's because I couldn't handle the thing with my mum, you know. I had to go to that clinic for two weeks.'

'Tell me more about your friendship with Marius.'

'He told me I shouldn't worry about the teasing. I had to become one of them. Group 13. Because they stick together. Last year I would often go home with him after school because his parents were never there during the day. It was nice. I could drink and smoke with him and he told me I was beautiful and he would see to it that I become important.'

'Drinking? During the day? And you're in standard eight only. What about your homework?'

The policeman's question irritates Engela. Does he also want to condemn her, just like the rest? She doesn't answer. She stares at an invisible point on the opposite wall.

'My dear child, it's okay if you open up and tell the sergeant everything,' her father had said three weeks ago. 'He's here to help you. He'll protect you against those nasty bastards.'

Geez, dad, she thought. Why are you never here to listen to me? You were never, ever there for me. But she was in a corner: Marius wanted to kill her, as he wrote in that letter.

'Tell me more about you and this . . . Group 13?'

Engela feels frustrated and tired. The policeman has been asking questions for an hour already since he brought her home. All she wants to do is go outside and have a cigarette under the tree. 'What else does Sergeant want to know?' she sighs.

'Everything. From the beginning.'

'I've told you how I met Marius.'

'Yes, but what about the rest of the gang?'

She will have to push on. It's either the policeman's questions or the death threats. She gets up, goes to the kitchen and pours herself a glass of Oros to suppress her craving for nicotine. A beer would be nice, actually. 'I became part of the group very quickly,' she says as she sits down again. She tries pulling her school skirt lower over her knees and takes a sip from the glass.

Pieterse doesn't move. He leans back quietly and observes her. 'And?'

'I don't know . . . things happened so fast after my mother's funeral I could hardly keep up. Before I realised what was going on I was part of the gang.'

'What did you guys do?'

'Played truant, often. Visiting at each other's houses. Here also. We drank a lot. We listened to heavy metal and burned each other . . .' She notices Pieterse doesn't understand. 'With cigarettes,' she explains. 'The group would hold the one down that had to be burned. And then Marius would put a cigarette out on that person's back.' She gets up, turns and pulls up her shirt. 'Look, there's my mark,' she points at her back.

Again Pieterse raises an eyebrow. 'And? What did you do then?'

'All sorts of crap. Tearing pages from the Bible and burning them. Writing on walls that Satan was the conqueror. Stuff like that. We also drew signs in our books and on our schoolbags.'

'Signs?'

'Satanic signs,' she says abruptly. What kind of a silly question is that? They both know why they are sitting in the lounge right now and why he has to take her to school and back every day.

'You felt at home with them?'

Yes, duhhh, she thinks. She presses her elbows down on her knees and lowers her face into her hands. 'You see, I felt . . . I felt like this group of people understood me . . . and it was probably because I was rebellious that I joined them. I told you I wanted to feel immortal. That's how I felt when I was with them. I wanted everybody else to leave me alone and be scared of me.'

'Where did you get the alcohol from?'

Engela lifts her head from her hands and looks at the policeman, dumbfounded. Where the hell do you get booze? 'At the bottle store,' she says sarcastically. She struggles to control her irritation.

'But you are minors . . .?'

'So what? That Porra doesn't care who he sells to.'

'With money you got where?'

'Stolen.'

Pieterse makes a note to question her later about the stealing. Engela can hear a car driving slowly past the house.

'This morning, on the way to school, you said something about the cemetery?'

'Yes?'

'Tell me about it?'

'There's nothing to tell, really. We would just go there sometimes. As a group. Usually on a Saturday night when everyone's parents had gone to bed. Then we would sneak out . . .' She pauses.

Pieterse motions for her to continue.

'Then . . . it was great fun. We kicked the fresh flowers from the graves. We painted the pentagram on the graves. We made promises to each other, that we would sacrifice everything for each other. We would stand together.'

Pieterse scribbles a few final words in his notebook before closing it. He glances at his watch. 'Gosh, look at the time. Four o'clock. And you still need to do your homework.'

Engela sighs with relief when he gets up and walks towards the door.

'See you tomorrow morning.'

'Yes, bye . . . fine . . .' Engela waves half-heartedly and quickly peeks out the front door. The street is quiet. Pieterse's Golf reverses out of the driveway and he drives off. Engela locks the door. In her bedroom she digs for the cigarettes in her schoolbag. She goes to the back yard and sits down under the tree. The match cracks over the striking surface. She inhales the first pull of nicotine and exhales the smoke delightedly. Suddenly she is calm, now that the policeman has gone and she can be alone with her cigarette under the tree. She has always had a connection with trees. These days, trees are where she hides when the noise in her head gets too much. When she was a toddler her mother would chain her to the tree outside their house in Brits when male friends came to visit while her father was away on army duty. She only starts to relax properly after the third pull. It was Marius and Group 13 that taught her how to smoke, swear and drink. Even at primary school she swore she would never, ever touch alcohol. It's what she thought every time she hid in her room when her parents started shouting at each other, throwing plates and sometimes punches. She would pull the pillow over her head, but she could still hear the fighting . . .

*   *   *

'You're a stupid quitter, man! Look at the mess we're in!' Dorothy shouts at her husband.

'And you? Since when are you such a great wife?' Andries retorts. 'Look at the house! And when last did you cook a proper meal? Hey? Hey?'

'Cooking! And with what money, if I may ask?'

'Oh please, don't start that crap again. I work my arse off in the army, but what do you do? Booze it all away and gallivant with your boyfriends when I'm away. Do you think I don't know about it?'

'Fuck you!'

The sound of a plate breaking against a wall tears through Engela's pillow.

'No, fuck you!'

More plates. More words. The seven-year-old pulls the pillow tighter around her head.

'Look around you. What do you see? A TV set? Furniture? No! Lewis took it all back because you didn't pay!'

The first punches fly. Engela starts sobbing; the pillow is no use. Intoxicated. The word she would eventually learn in standard six at Fichardt Park High. And she will never, ever be intoxicated in her entire life, she would write in her school essay. But the thing with Marius and Group 13 and her mother has made a lie of that essay.

Outside, under the tree, Engela tries to remember her mum, but the memories aren't very clear. Earlier this year, when the doctor at the clinic prescribed some pills, he said it would help to take away the memories and the pain for a while. And when the memories returned it would hurt less, he said. Engela drops the cigarette butt on the ground next to her. She lights up the next one immediately. She wants to remember the way her mother was. That day, Tuesday, 9 February. All she remembers now is the blood. The entire room was covered in blood.

Then there's a car again, passing slowly in the street. This time, however, it stops in front of the house. She's scared all of a sudden. She puts the cigarette out next to the previous butt and walks cautiously to the back door. Maybe the policeman came back, she tries to convince herself. She peeps out the lounge window. Marius du Preez is standing on the pavement behind the fence, a foot resting on the bottom rail, his left arm on the pillar. When he spots her in the window he sneers. He lifts his right hand and draws an outstretched finger across his throat before turning around and getting back into the car.

Engela gets the message: they are coming to kill her.

Three

The Ster-Kinekor cinema on Hoffman Square in Bloemfontein is packed. One of the best movies of 1993 thus far, was how movie critic Leon van Nierop had praised Steven Spielberg's *Schindler's List* when it opened on circuit in South Africa the previous week. Pieter didn't really enjoy the epic drama, but at least he felt safe during the movie's three-hour running time. He's been living in fear for the past month. He knows Anthony's guys are tracking him. Mark wants his Porsche or his money back.

'Don't screw with me. Don't even try. You won't know what hit you. Understood?' Mark had warned him three months ago. But Pieter still has no Porsche to show for it, and no money to hand back. After the film Pieter stays in a crowd of people as they step onto the pavement.

Don't worry, my contact stole a car in the Netherlands, Pieter had lied six weeks ago when he reported back to the club. The lies flowed with the alcohol: the vehicle will be shipped to Durban, taken to a chop shop for a makeover and a new engine number, and then sent on to Welkom. Everything was under control; he had a contact in every spot, Pieter assured them. But he needed another R3 000 advance; his contacts wanted their money upfront, he explained.

Hell, at least he tried, Pieter thought to himself as Mark slowly counted the notes on the coffee table in front of him. He really tried. For some time now he's been in cahoots with a local guy who deals in stolen car radios, and who got him the number of a gang leader on the Cape Flats. The gangster would help him, but asked for R1 000 upfront, only to disappear like a needle in a haystack. Maybe he should just return Mark's money and forget about the whole thing, Pieter thought. How on earth was he supposed to get the R1 000 back? He saw his salvation in the Thaba Nchu casino, about an hour's drive from the city, but the one-armed bandits took his money as fast as the gangster did. To win big you have to play big. He had read this free advice from a professional gambler from Las Vegas in an advertisement. For $100 you could order the complete secrets to casino success and wealth. That's why Pieter had asked for an extra R3 000 six weeks ago: to order the professional gambler's manual and to have funds to go to the Thaba Nchu casino and gamble Mark's money back. But the professional gambler's recipe turned out to be exactly what it claimed to be: a secret. It didn't work for Pieter.

Outside on the pavement the cinemagoers are breaking up into small groups as they walk to their parked vehicles. Pieter takes a left to where he had parked some distance from the Spur. In front of him a couple, very much in love, walk arm in arm; right behind him are five students, giggling. Thank goodness, he thinks with relief as he pushes the key into the car door lock a few moments later.

'Hi, Pieter. Enjoyed the movie?'

Pieter jumps. It's Steve's voice. He pushes Pieter away from the car door, locks it and puts the key in his pocket.

'How about a nightcap, hey? Come.'

Steve doesn't wait for Pieter to reply. He grips his upper arm tightly as they walk across the square, passing a police van from Park Station that's parked in front of the Spur. The last municipal bus of the evening pulls away with six passengers on board. Steve doesn't make small talk. They go past the Sanlam Mall and then up Oos Burger Street all the way to Lady Femmé. Jacques opens the trellis gate from the reception area with his remote control. George is behind the bar counter pouring drinks for a group of men having a good time. There are three girls with them. In the office Anthony sits in the black leather chair next to the big desk. Steve sits down in the other chair.

'You've got problems, right?' Anthony asks. His usual smile is gone, as well as his customary offer of a drink. Pieter keeps quiet. He remains standing in front of the door that was closed behind him.

'It seems to me that you . . . how shall I put it . . . screwed up?' Anthony hisses like a puff adder about to strike. Then he roars as he suddenly gets up: 'Answer me, fuckit!'

Pieter can't stay upright. Trembling, he walks towards the edge of the couch, where he sits down. His eyes avoid Anthony, who is pacing the room threateningly.

'Are you going to deliver?' Anthony lights himself a cigar. 'You're not as assertive as you used to be, right? Have you hit the big silence?' He tips ash into the ashtray. 'Okay, you don't feel like talking, it seems. Then I'll speak.'

'I can explain—' Pieter stammers.

'Wow. You can explain. In this game we're not looking for explanations, pal. We want delivery.'

'I—'

'Shut up. You came walking in here with a bunch of stories.

About your contacts. You who can organise and do anything. Remember? I believed you. You came drinking at my expense and took two girls to the rooms. At my expense, because I believed you. I introduced you to Mark. It was a small job. Stealing a bloody car and giving it a makeover is a small job.' Anthony pours himself another Cognac to calm down. 'Mark . . . Mark was a small job. He wants his car, Pieter, or his money back. I introduced him to you but now he wants to bite your head off. And you are definitely not dropping me. Understood?'

Pieter nods. He desperately needs a drink, but there's no way he can ask for one right now.

Anthony sits down again. 'I'm glad you understand. So, let's get to the point. First question: Is Mark's Porsche on the way, like you promised?'

Pieter stares at the carpet. He shakes his head. There's no point in lying; he's been caught out.

'I see . . . I see.' Anthony lights another cigar. He resumes his pacing as the smoke whirls behind him. 'Shit!' he yells suddenly and bangs his fist against the couch. He sits down. He doesn't say anything, just stares at Pieter. Steve also stares at him from the other side of the room.

'I want the advance. Tomorrow morning – R7 000 plus interest, because you wasted our time,' Anthony says after he's calmed down a bit. 'I'll send George around. Nick's Auto Repairs, we know where that is. Be sure the money is waiting: R8 000, in notes.'

Pieter still says nothing. Just keeps staring at the carpet as if it's the strangest thing he's ever seen. Anthony waves his hand towards the door. 'Get out of here.'

'There is one more thing . . .' Pieter says reluctantly.

'Yes?' Anthony asks when Pieter pauses.

'The money . . . I . . . I don't have it.'

30

'Holy shit! HOLY SHIT! And just how do you think you are going to pay back Mark's money? Hey? How?'

'I . . . I don't know.'

'What? You don't know? You don't know?'

Pieter nods. Anthony paces the room, fuming. He lets rip a swear word now and then. Then he walks up to Pieter. 'You are in big trouble, pal. Big trouble, I tell you. Mark is nobody's playmate.'

There is another round of swearing before an eerie silence fills the room. The club owner tops up Anthony's glass and sits down. From the bar comes the sound of music pumping. Occasionally laughter can be heard over the music. By now Pieter knows every pattern and thread in the carpet by heart. 'I didn't mean to—'

'Shut up!' Anthony silences him.

It's not like he deceived them on purpose, Pieter tries to make himself feel better. He just wanted to be in with the big guys. The big shots. And he wanted to make money. Lots of money. More than his pathetic salary and the profit he gains from the car radios he swings. What is so difficult about that? He might have pulled it off had that trash from the Cape Flats not cheated him . . .

'I'll make you a deal. I'll save your arse,' Anthony says some time later.

Pieter looks at Anthony for the first time. Thank goodness, it seems there might be a way out of this, he thinks. Anthony walks over and sits down on top of the coffee table, his face close to Pieter's. Pieter can smell the Cognac and cigar smoke clinging to Anthony's words. He stresses every word as he spells out his deal to Pieter. He'll talk to Mark. Coax him with a couple of favours from the club's side. He will also pay the money back out of his own pocket, but he wants something in return. If Pieter can pull this off they'll forget about this entire mess and Pieter can continue as before. Without fear.

'What . . . what is it . . . you want in return?' Pieter asks when the man in front of him stops talking.

The Cognac-and-cigar voice gets up close to Pieter's face. Then he whispers in his ear. One sentence, one sentence only. Pieter can feel the blood rushing from his head. His hands are shaking. No, he can't, he wants to shout. But Anthony gets up and opens the door. 'Screw this up, friend, and you can forward your measurements to AVBOB.'

Four

Sergeant Pieterse observes Engela as she plays with the pen in her hand. She puts it down on the small table in the centre of the lounge, but picks it up again after a few moments. She keeps turning the pen while she talks. Every now and then she lifts her head and looks out the window. She hasn't told the policeman about Marius du Preez's visit yesterday. If she does he will go and confront him. And then she'll be in even deeper trouble.

'Nervous?' Pieterse asks.

'A little stressed out . . . exams . . .' she dodges the question.

Pieterse laughs. 'Yes, I felt the same way when I was at school. Later in life we realise exams are not as bad as we thought they were when we were at school.'

You're just talking crap, Engela thinks and peeps outside again. She can't stand the fear. It's not only her life that's threatened, but also that of her dad and her stepmother, Susan. They won't leave the old folks alone, she knows.

'I won't be long, then you can go study,' she hears the policeman say. 'Let's focus today only on what happened at Naval Hill.'

Engela nods.

'It was last month, right?'

She nods again.

'Date?'

She tells him and he writes it down in his notebook: Friday, 2 July 1993.

'How did it start?'

'Marius told us about it the previous weekend. We had a party at his house. He said he had planned everything for all the newcomers. Said it was going to be a wonderful weekend. Out of town all the way to the city. We would assemble at Naval Hill. We'll be learning amazing things, he said. Because it's the place where the Satanists hang out. We had to pack our bags that Friday and meet up at his house.'

'How many of you?'

'Three. Lizmarie, Brenda and I. Marius didn't go with.'

'And your parents? How did you get past them?'

'We lied to them. You know, the staying-over-at-a-friend's excuse. My dad and auntie Susan never even checked anyway.'

'Right. So then you're at Marius' place. And then?'

'It was the Friday night after the previous Saturday's party when Marius chose us. Yes, we drank at first. A lot. Then this other dude turns up. His name's Wayne and he and Marius were pals. He came to fetch us. He was older than us . . . finished with school. He was big and tall. He wore a black cape that made him look even taller. Then he said a prayer and drank with us.'

Pieterse lifts his eyebrows. 'A prayer?'

'Yes. For Satan. Then we left. It was dark by the time we reached Bloemfontein. We went straight to Naval Hill. It's a . . . a hill in the city centre . . .'

'Okay,' Pieterse interrupts her. 'I know it. What happened next?'

'We parked at the top of the hill. There were other cars also. And a lot of people hanging about. There were tents also. I think some of the people stayed the night. Everybody was older than us. We didn't know anyone, but I wasn't afraid. It was quite exciting, actually. Candles were burning everywhere. More people arrived and we hung out and drank. Then much later . . . I can't remember exactly what time . . . maybe around eleven or so, somebody said it was time, we had to go.'

'Somebody?'

'Can't remember his name. But he was one of the leaders. He was wearing a long, black cape . . . we followed him . . .'

The pen twirls in Engela's hand. Then she taps it on her leg for a while before putting it down on the table. The policeman makes notes incessantly. She gets up and goes to the kitchen. Her throat is sore from all the talking and she has a funny feeling in her belly.

After that Friday night the pregnant girl on Naval Hill appears frequently in her dreams. She yells and pulls at the blanket and tries to suffocate her. On a few occasions Engela has woken her dad and stepmother with her screaming; then they come to her room with a glass of water and console her.

'Another bad dream?' her dad wants to know.

Engela takes sips of water through the tears.

The pregnant girl . . .

She never told her folks about the pregnant girl, or about Naval Hill. This afternoon she's talking about it for the first time. With the policeman in the lounge making notes all the time. The leader in the black cape led them to an open spot in the field. A large pentagram was painted on the ground, with red and black candles burning on each corner. They stood in a circle around it. Everyone was holding a candle. The girl was kneeling in the centre of the circle. Her upper body was naked, almost defenceless, her belly showing she was six months gone. The candlelight painted strange patterns over her full breasts, Engela remembers. Breasts that would soon be nurturing her baby.

Pieterse notices the red glow in Engela's eyes when she returns from the kitchen with a glass of water, but he doesn't say anything.

'Everyone was making these strange noises . . . like they were praying, but in a foreign language. In the centre of the circle . . . inside the sign . . . the girl . . . there were three glasses filled with blood next to her. In front of her, on the ground, there were knives . . .'

Engela takes a sip of the water. She wipes the back of her hand across her eyes. She imagines hearing a car again. She looks outside, but it's just Pieterse's Golf parked in front of the house. 'You know, I have dreams about these things, over and over. Over and over!' She slams the glass of water down on the table.

'And then?' Pieterse continues after she has composed herself.

'Then . . . another leader . . . also wearing a long cape . . . pulled over his face, I couldn't see it, walked up to the girl, stood in front of her . . . offered her one of the glasses filled with blood to drink. Somebody next to me said she was going to sacrifice her child to Satan. Suddenly I could see the evil spirits. They were everywhere, all around me. I started screaming . . .'

'Evil spirits?'

'Yes . . . these creatures that were hovering in the air . . . all around us.' I was hysterical. I just wanted to get away, but some of the people pushed me down to the ground and gagged me. I bit one of the guys' hands . . . I remember the blood in my mouth. I don't know how it happened . . . I mean, where I got the strength from, but I managed to free myself and ran away.'

'And no one chased you? Tried to stop you, or catch you?'

'Two of the leaders ran after me, but I was too quick for them. I hid in a bush. A group with flashlights also walked past me, but didn't see me under the bush. I started running again when they were gone. All the way down the mountain path. There were dogs barking everywhere . . . along the path. These huge, gaunt dogs in cages . . . they were jumping up against the cages, trying to bite me.'

'These dogs . . . were they also evil spirits?'

Engela nods. 'I think so. But I don't know really. It was horrendous. I just had to get away. I ran and ran all the way down. Then down the road until I reached the swimming pool.'

'The Arthur Nathan?'

'Yes. It must have been after midnight, but there was this young couple in a car at the entrance, they were . . . making out. I knocked against the window and pleaded for a lift. They dropped me on the N1.'

'That was when you hitchhiked home?'

'Yes . . .'

Pieterse closes his notebook. 'That's enough for today. You still have your homework. I'll see you tomorrow?'

'Fine.'

Engela goes back to the willow tree outside when the policeman's gone. She lights a cigarette. Only then do the tears come and take control of her. Will 1993's crying never stop . . .?

* * *

The girl with the baby inside her is standing on her knees. Her head sways from side to side. She's mumbling something, but Engela can't make it out. The girl takes the glass from the leader. Engela wants to shout at her not to take it, but there's no sound coming from her throat. The blood runs down the girl's mouth. Engela wants to run to her, but three men push her to the ground. The dogs are barking. They're jumping up and down next to her. Engela struggles to free herself, but one of the guys presses down on her throat with his arm. She kicks at the dogs trying to bite her. She struggles to breathe. The dogs are slobbering over her face. The rotten smell burns her nose. She screams . . .

Engela wakes up. The blankets are pulled over her head. She kicks them off and sits up straight, shaking. Outside she can hear the neighbour's dog barking. Her hand reaches out for the bedside lamp switch. It's just gone midnight, she can see from the clock. She gets up and walks quietly to the bathroom through the dark house. From the main bedroom she can hear her dad and stepmom in a deep sleep. She flushes the toilet and drinks water from the basin tap. In the lounge she peeps through the window to see what the dog is barking at. There's no one in the street, but the dog is barking furiously. She turns on the outside light to get a better view; maybe it will calm the dog down as well, she thinks. She goes outside. Only then does she see the long, black object hanging from the front gate. She moves closer. It's a cat. Blood is dripping from the gaping hole where its head once was.

Five

'Beer?' Barry asks when Engela enters the workshop in Oranjesig just after five.

'Please!' She drops her handbag on the floor dejectedly and falls into the dirty plastic chair in the corner. Barry appears from underneath a car bonnet, wipes his hands on his overalls and takes a Castle from the six-pack in the Solly Kramer's bag sitting on top of the workbench against the wall.

Nick's Auto Repairs closed fifteen minutes ago. It's just Barry and Pieter in the workshop, and two admin girls in the office. The rest of the staff have gone home already. Outside, the peak-hour traffic in Church Street snails towards Bloemfontein's eastern suburbs.

'Cheers,' Barry says, taking a sip from an already half-empty can.

'Yeah, whatever.'

'Nothing today?' he asks his sister, who's seven years younger than him.

She shakes her head.

'Oh well, tomorrow's another day.' He takes a number 4

spanner from the shelf and busies himself with the engine. 'Just want to finish this and then we can go.'

Pieter slides out from under another vehicle. 'Hi,' he nods in Engela's direction and gets himself a beer. 'I'll also keep my ears open for something.'

The two guys chat about spare parts to be ordered the next day, but she doesn't listen to them. She wonders why her dad hasn't called even once. She knew she had to escape after the episode with the dead cat three weeks ago. She didn't say a word to Sergeant Pieterse on the way to school that Friday morning. After he had dropped her off, she turned around and ran straight home. She did things as fast as she could: packed a suitcase, wrote a note to her dad that she left on the kitchen table, and then proceeded to the café, where she made a collect call to her brother in Bloemfontein. It's not like they have the traditional brother-sister relationship, but he was the only one she could go to. She also had a bit of luck that day: the sixth car that passed her as she was hitchhiking gave her a lift. The greater the distance she put between herself, Dewetsdorp and Group 13, the lighter her mood became. Now her life was awaiting her, the sixteen-year-old thought. She would quickly find a job in the city, move into a nice flat and everything would be a big party. After an hour's drive she was dropped off on the N1 at the Jagersfontein off-ramp. She walked the remaining four kilometres to Barry's and Miems' two-bedroom flat.

'Let's go,' Barry says and throws the empty beer can in the dustbin. Since she has been around the past three weeks they don't talk much on the way back to his flat in the afternoons. But today, just before they enter the complex, he says: 'You know you can't stay here forever, right? You'll have to make a plan.'

Go to hell. You're a cold, callous pig, she thinks. Actually, she has always hated her brother. Well, maybe not always. There was a time, before she started school, when they were still living in Brits, that she looked up to him. When their parents started their drunken arguing in the lounge she would sometimes flee to his bedroom. He was her brother, he would protect her, she thought for a long time when she was a toddler. But he chased her out every time. The hate only came much later, after they moved to Bloemfontein in 1984. She remembers very well the year the hate took control of her heart. It was 1987. She was ten years old, in standard three, and he was seventeen. That was when she would go with him to his high school teacher's plot outside the city. Later, she would beg him not to take her along, but he forced her. That was when the hate sprouted, and it eventually grew as lush as the bushes on the plot.

When she made that collect call, three weeks ago, it was his wife, Miems, who answered and said it was fine, that she could stay a couple of days. But the couple of days continued for much longer than she had anticipated.

'Yes, I know,' is all Engela says when they get out of the car and walk towards the flat. She feels a little light-headed from the two beers she has downed. She feels the tears burning her eyes. Why is it so difficult to find a job? Every morning, for three weeks already, she has driven with her brother to the workshop. Then she takes the bus to Hoffman Square and tackles the city armed with the one-page CV that Miems typed out and photocopied for her. She walks from store to store. 'Please sir, anything,' she repeats the words as she moves along. Then the usual strange expression in the managers' eyes and the heads that shake from side to side. No, nothing here. Not for a child. The guy at Checkers in the Sanlam Mall opposite Loch Logan reacted in the same way.

'Please, sir, even if it is behind the till.'

'Maybe you should rather go back to school,' he mocked her.

But seven days ago her age didn't bother the Greek dude at the Westdene Café and Takeaways in Barnes Street. Yes, for R4.50 an hour she could help out in the afternoons. There were flats above the café. She'd be moving in there in a month's time, Engela had thought excitedly. But after three days the Greek chased her away. She couldn't add, he said.

Barry goes to his bedroom soon after dinner. He's tired and doesn't feel like their chitchat, he's off to bed, he mumbles. Engela and Miems sit in the lounge drinking Tassenberg that Miems taps from a five-litre box. Miems is all right, Engela thinks. She just can't get why Miems would marry a pig like her brother. Suddenly the cheap red wine makes the tears run down her cheeks. 'I know I can't stay here forever, Miems, I know . . .'

'It's fine, don't worry, things will get better,' her sister-in-law consoles her.

'You know what, sis, I'm upset with myself actually. For this mess I'm in. And dad and them. And now you guys have to put up with me. I wish I could turn back the clock . . . I blame myself for what I have done. If it wasn't for Group 13. If I hadn't gone to Naval Hill that Friday night . . . if . . . if . . . things could have been so different . . .'

Miems doesn't say anything. Engela keeps talking, the words oozing from her wound. Her life is like a boil, she thinks. 'I know it sounds silly, but if I had known a couple of months ago what was going to happen . . . I mean the consequences . . . I never would have gone to Naval Hill that night. I mean . . . I wouldn't even have befriended Marius and the gang. And now that they are on my case . . . I mean, I know what they wanted to do to me. And dad and Auntie Susan . . . they could have been hurt also . . . that's the way the group operates. I know.'

She puts her empty glass down on the table. 'I had to flee, Miems. I had to.'

'It's all right, Engela, I said it's okay.' Miems consoles her again and pours them more wine.

'I miss my mum . . . every day I wish it was only a dream . . . all the blood in the room . . . that it was only a dream . . . that she's not dead . . . that she's still alive . . . I'm scared, Miems, I'm flippen scared . . .'

Engela scratches in her handbag for a tissue. She staggers to the bathroom and blows her nose. Her feet ache from walking door to door the whole day. 'Geez, I don't know any more,' she sobs as she sits down again and takes another gulp of wine. 'If only I can find a job. Like all those people getting off the buses at the square every morning on their way to work. Why doesn't anyone want to employ me, sis? I just want to make my own life. It's not too much to ask, is it?'

As she sits there crying on the couch, with her legs pulled up under her, suddenly she is no longer the rebellious teenager who has run away from home. The wine has turned her into a little girl afraid of life. A little girl longing for her mother. 'Maybe we can go to the grave on Saturday?' she asks through the tears.

Miems nods her head. She's too drunk to speak.

The next morning Engela is woken by the sound of the telephone ringing in the lounge. Outside it's still a little dark. Sounds like rain. It's quiet inside the flat – just the phone ringing and ringing. Confused, she wonders why no one is getting it. Her mouth tastes of red wine and tears and her head aches. She can hear someone going down the passage and answering the phone. She can hear her brother's voice. Only then does she remember where she is. She's still too confused to make out what he is saying, but moments later he opens her bedroom door. Without knocking, like he always does. He leans against the doorframe. 'Pieter called,' he says without greeting her. 'He says he knows of a job for you. You should pack your suitcase. He'll take you there tonight.'

Six

'What's wrong?' Engela asks when Pieter suddenly slows down.

'Nothing. Just careful in the rain.'

Swoosh, swoosh, the wipers clear the water from the windscreen. This has been her worst year for crying, ever, Engela thinks. From now on she's never going to cry again. Tonight she gets a job and then things will be fine. 'What kind of work is it? Do you know?' she asks again.

'Nothing difficult. Like I said, screw these other guys who didn't want to employ you. You'll see.'

Engela is happy and excited. 'But is it office work or a big business? Come on, Pieter. Tell me.'

'All I know is you'll be making lots of money . . . lots and lots of money.'

'And eventually start my new life.'

'Exactly.'

'Why did I have to pack my suitcase, Pieter?'

'Because you'll be staying there. They supply food and a bed, so you don't have to bother going back to Barry's place every night. That's why.'

'Ah! With my first salary I'm going to find myself a flat and buy nice things. Will you come help me move in and arrange things? I don't feel like asking Barry.'

'Of course I'll come help you.'

'Then we'll have a big party.'

'With lots of champagne.'

Engela laughs. After Barry woke her this morning, she jumped out of bed with a huge hangover, packed her suitcase, said goodbye to Miems and drove with her brother to Nick's Auto Repairs. She left her things in his car, went into town and walked around the shops. This time she wasn't looking for a job; this time her eyes touched on the bedding, ornaments and furniture for her new place. By five o'clock she was back at the workshop. Barry, his hands covered in grease, was still busy trying to get a client's vehicle to start, but Pieter was in a hurry. Brother and sister said their brief goodbyes with a simple wave.

'I just want to stop by my flat quickly,' Pieter said as they left. 'You can wait in the car.' When he reappeared, his dirty overall had been exchanged for a pair of jeans and an open-neck shirt. Important people, he explained; one has to look respectable.

'How much money?' Engela asks as Pieter turns into St Andrew's Street before the square.

'A lot. More than you could ever dream of.'

'Geez,' she claps her hands with excitement, 'I can't wait.'

At the ticket booth in front of Ster-Kinekor people are queueing on the pavement. She'll come watch a movie after work every night, Engela decides. They never used to have money for movies. Or milkshakes. Pieter turns left into Fichardt Street and left again into Charles after two blocks. He slows down, enters an alleyway and stops in front of a steel gate. 'Is this the place?' Engela asks.

He ignores her and presses the intercom outside the car.

'Lady Femmé,' a voice says. 'How can we help?'

'Hi, Anthony. It's Pieter.'

The gate opens and shuts immediately behind them. Pieter parks next to a white Mercedes under a canopy.

'Come,' he commands. She steps out of the car. He takes the suitcase from the back seat and pushes it into her hands. A big red arrow flashes 'ENTRANCE' against the wall, but Pieter continues to a door at the back of the building.

'Are you sure I'll be allowed to stay here tonight?' she asks.

'Don't worry. They will give you a place to sleep, food and clothes. Just come along.'

Okay, that's great, Engela thinks and follows Pieter. He knocks. A tall guy with blond hair opens the door. Come inside, he says and stands to the side. She sees a small kitchen. Somewhere music is playing.

Pieter offers a hand but the blond guy doesn't take it. Pieter lowers his hand. 'This is Engela.'

Anthony looks her up and down. 'Nice, very nice,' he says after a while. Only then does he smile and put his hand out to Pieter. 'Well done. You can go now.'

Pieter turns and leaves without saying goodbye. Anthony locks the door and the security gate and puts his arm around Engela's shoulder. 'Put your suitcase down here by the kitchen cupboard and come with me,' he says, with a gesture. She walks with him to the bar, where the music is coming from.

'Sit,' he says and motions to the row of stools in front of the bar counter.

'Where am I?' she asks hesitantly, looking around. There's no one else in the bar. 'Are we alone?'

'Yup. We only open at eight. Relax. We'll look after you nicely.'

'Is . . . this . . . my new place of work?

'Yup! Looks nice, doesn't it? We have a lot of fun in here.' He puts a drink down in front of her.

She takes a sip. She tastes the Coke, but there's something unfamiliar mixed with it. 'What's this?'

'A welcome drink. Free and on the house, of course.'

He lifts his own glass in her direction. 'Cheers. And welcome.'

'Cheers. Am I allowed to smoke?'

'Of course,' Anthony says and offers her a cigar.

'No, thanks, I have my own.' The unfamiliar surroundings make her nervous all of a sudden. The packet of Benson & Hedges shakes a little in her hand as she takes it out of her handbag. She can feel perspiration on her forehead and her throat tightening. She takes two big sips from her drink. 'What kind of work will I be doing?' She points at the bar. 'Will I be working in here?' The big clock on the wall shows half past seven. The customers will probably start arriving soon.

Anthony shakes his head. 'Not in here. Your place of work is down the passage.'

Engela turns and notices a door behind the pool table. She feels a little dizzy. Must be because of the lack of fresh air. There isn't a window or a fan in sight. She empties her glass. Then it all goes dark in front of her.

*   *   *

'No, Barry, please, I don't want to go again!' Engela screams.

'You better come along!' Barry shouts back. 'You know he gives us food. Or do you want us to die from hunger, hey?'

She is in standard three at Fichardt Park Primary and he's in standard nine in high school.

'I don't want to, I don't want to! You know, Barry! I don't want to any more!' Now she's resisting, but earlier that year when they went to Barry's mathematics teacher's plot in Bainsvlei for the first time, it was nice. Her tiny heart was beating fast when Mr de Wet stopped outside their house that Saturday morning in his blue Nissan Skyline to pick up the two children. She could hear their mother pouring herself something in the kitchen to get her going. Usually gin and Oros. Or cane and milk if there were no soft drinks in the house. She's happy to get out of the house today. When her mother starts pouring this early it means she'll be drunk by eleven o'clock. Her dad is working and won't be home for the weekend, which means her mother will probably be having her male friends over later on. Then it's stuff for grown-ups and she will have to play outside. Should she talk back she'll get chained to the tree.

Mr de Wet inserts a cassette into the player on the dashboard and turns up the volume. Engela recognises the song when Atlantic Starr sings 'We both know that we should not be together'.

Mr de Wet looks in the rear-view mirror and smiles at her. She returns the smile. They drive along Jagersfontein Road towards the N1 and then north all the way to the Kimberley off-ramp. They pass Langenhoven Park, crossing at the big intersection until there are no more buildings along the road.

'Almost there,' he says.

He turns off onto a gravel road at the Bainsvlei smallholdings. Moments later, he stops the car in front of a huge iron gate.

'Please, will you open the gate for us, Barry?' he asks and pushes a set of keys into Barry's hand. 'This one,' he says and points at a key. Barry jumps out, runs to the gate and fiddles with the key in the padlock. Then the gate swings open and he stands back for them to pass through. Mr de Wet parks the car in front of a small house with a red tin roof and a stoep. A bakkie is parked next to the house under a car port. Further away, Engela spots a paddock with three horses.

'Let's have refreshments before the day starts,' he says as he invites them into the house. 'It's getting hot already.'

Maybe her brother loves her after all, Engela thinks as she finds herself with a cool drink on the couch in the lounge a little later. Last night he invited her to come along to the plot. Usually he chases her from his bedroom when she's looking for attention or simply wants to escape when their parents are at each other's throats again in the lounge. Now he and the teacher are talking about car issues. Barry has to service the bakkie, she realises. Barry knows about car engines, Engela thinks with pride. Even when he was little, those days in Brits, he would get underneath cars and teach himself. It was his way of escaping when things got too much inside the house. He never said much, just went outside and buried his head under one of the broken-down cars in the yard. They never had proper automobiles. When there was money their father would purchase an old piece of crap that they would drive until it broke down. Barry would then try to get it running again on the weekends. Sometimes he succeeded, sometimes not. Then the car would stay right there in the yard. Once there were three wrecks on their property in Brits, Engela recalls.

'Little girl, we can't be sitting around all day,' she hears Mr de Wet say all of a sudden. 'Let's go see what the horses are up to.'

They go outside and Barry disappears round the side of the house where the bakkie is parked. She can hear the bonnet opening behind her. Mr de Wet talks about all sorts of stuff as they walk to the paddock, but she's not really listening.

She looks at the chickens scratching close to the fence. Must be nice being a chicken, she thinks. There's food always, and nobody fights with you. Mr de Wet busies himself with the horses. He separates one of them and chases it into the stable. She stands at the stable door and observes as he puts a saddle on the horse's back and fastens the straps under the animal's belly. He peeps at her over his shoulder.

'You're a cute little girl, you know,' he says, winking at her.

'Thanks, sir,' she responds, embarrassed, and stares at the ground. Doesn't he see the old, faded clothes she's wearing, she wonders. Doesn't it bother him? Her blouse with the flower pattern and the white buttons fits just a little too tight. Part of her stomach shows just above her shorts. The plastic flip-flops make her feet sweat in the stable. Her toes are already dirty from the dust, she notices when she looks down.

'Your brother said you were pretty, but I never imagined you would be this pretty.'

What? Did Barry say she was pretty? Engela's heart skips a beat with excitement, and then she blushes. 'Thank you, sir . . .'

'Are we going for a short ride?'

'I don't know, sir . . . I've never ridden a horse before.'

'Come on. You'll enjoy it, you'll see.'

'But what if I fall down? I don't know how to ride.'

'Don't worry. You sit in the saddle in front of me and I'll hold you. You'll be safe. You'll see. Come say hello.'

'What's his name?' she asks as she approaches the horse carefully.

'Satan. Come, rub his head.'

'Why Satan, sir?' Engela lifts an arm but she can't reach the horse's head. He turns away.

'Because he's so big and fast. And black.'

He pulls the reins over the animal's head and fastens them.

Satan resists. 'Easy, easy now, Satan,' Mr de Wet coaxes. He leads the horse from the stable and Engela stands aside. She looks on as he puts his left foot into the stirrup and swings his body over the horse's back.

'Stay here.' he calls over his shoulder. He shakes the reins against the horse's neck and spurs him on with his heels. There's a cloud of dust as Satan takes off at a fast gallop and heads for the entrance gate to the plot. Mr de Wet steers him past the gate, pulling the reins to the right as the two of them head down the road. That looks nice, Engela thinks, as her eyes follow them. Just before the gravel road reaches the main road, horse and rider turn around and charge back. Moments later, Satan halts in front of the stable, neighing, and Mr de Wet gets down.

'Come, get on,' he beckons. Engela moves closer to the gigantic animal. Mr de Wet puts his arms around her waist. 'Jump!' he says and lifts her onto the horse before he joins her.

'It's really high, sir.'

'We'll go slowly, I promise.'

He grips the reins and allows the horse to walk only. The pommel of the saddle hurts between her legs and she shifts slightly to the back. Mr de Wet presses her tightly against him.

'See, it's nice.'

'Yes, sir,' is all she can mutter.

Satan trots out the gate and left along the gravel road. The sun is hot on her face and legs. It's much better here than at home. Here it's calm and there's no arguing. There are also no schoolkids mocking her.

'Having fun?' she hears Mr de Wet's voice behind her.

She nods. 'Yes, sir.'

'Will you come visit again?'

'Yes, sir.'

His hand brushes lightly over her thigh. Later, when they're back, he shows her how to cool Satan down and then how to brush him. She stands on a stool in the stable and pulls the brush with even strokes across the horse's body. His muscles contract. She finds it peculiar. Mr de Wet is busy dishing out bales of hay to the other horses. Then he cleans the water trough and adds fresh water.

'When we're done here you can go and have a nice hot bath,' he says as he hangs the stable fork against the wall.

Engela is startled. Does she smell? She had a bath on Wednesday night, but without soap because there was no more in the house. On top of that the municipality cut off their electricity on Thursday morning, but her mother said they would make a plan to pay the arrears after the weekend and then it would be restored. That evening she dunked her face cloth in cold water and wiped her face. She's used to it, but the teasing at school she'll never get used to. 'Stinky, you smell rotten, man!' some of the children would tease her when there was no more soap, shampoo or hot water at home. When the army minibus dropped her dad off yesterday afternoon he was carrying a couple of two-litre bottles of Paarl Perlé. No soap or shampoo. No food, either.

'Let's go inside. We're done here,' Mr de Wet says.

Engela slips on her dirty flip-flops and walks half a pace behind the teacher to the house.

'How are you coming along?' he asks Barry.

Barry appears from underneath the bonnet of the bakkie. There are spots of oil on his forehead, Engela notices. She wonders if he will also be allowed to take a bath.

'Fine, sir. Just the spark plugs and a bit of tuning and then it'll be okay. But you will have to let someone take a look at the steering bracket.'

'Another day,' says Mr de Wet. 'When you're done, go have a look in the shed and load a pumpkin and a bag of maize for you guys.'

'Wow, thank you, sir,' Barry says and starts undoing the old spark plugs.

'We'll see you inside a little later. I'm going to make some boerewors rolls.'

Engela's stomach is pining for food. She knows Barry was given some food last night by people in the neighbourhood whose windscreen wipers he had replaced, but the last thing she had eaten was a sandwich at school yesterday morning. Her Afrikaans teacher had brought it for her.

Inside Mr de Wet runs a hot bath. 'Come, I've added some foam bath. You did a good job in the stables today.'

Engela nods. She's still too shy to speak in full sentences. The foam bath smells sweet. Mr de Wet closes the door behind him and busies himself in the kitchen. Engela kicks off her flip-flops, undoes the white buttons on her blouse and takes it off. Her shorts land on her blouse, then her panties. Her mother hasn't bought her a bra yet, even though her youthful curves could do with one. Her dirty toes test the water before she gets in. Then she stretches out in the tub. The foam bubbles on her skin. Geez, this is smart, she thinks. In two months she'll be ten years old. On 30 May 1987. If anyone asks about a gift for her she'll say she'd like a bottle of these bath bubbles. She will hide it deep in her wardrobe so no one can get to it. Only she will bath in it, she lies there thinking.

The bathroom door clicks open. Suddenly Mr de Wet is standing in front of the bathtub, staring at her. He is holding a red towel. She doesn't know what to do, but instinctively she crosses her arms over her chest.

'Sorry,' he says, 'I forgot to bring you a towel.' He puts the towel down on the toilet seat, but his eyes are fixed on the parts of her naked body visible above the water. Engela tries sinking even lower.

'Hell, you are pretty,' he says before he turns around and leaves.

That was the first Saturday on the teacher's plot in Bains-vlei, the year she was in standard three. After that she and her brother would go there more and more, at least one Saturday in the month. And every time Mr de Wet dropped them at their house there was food. Pumpkin, gem squash, mealies, melon, green beans, onions or whatever he was harvesting from his vegetable patch that month. There were also little gifts for her: a new pair of flip-flops, a T-shirt, deodorant or perfume. Two months later she also received the birthday gift she dreamt about that first Saturday in the bathtub. The bottle of bath bubbles. Because a nice girl like you should always look and smell nice, he would always say. It was only towards the end of that year of 1987 that she didn't want to go to the plot any more.

'No, Barry, I don't want to go!' Engela screamed.

'You better come along!' Barry shouted back. 'You know we get food. Or do you want us to die from hunger, hey?'

'I don't want to, I don't want to! You know, Barry! I don't want to go there any more!' The pain was getting too much for her.

* * *

I don't want to, Barry, I don't want to, Engela moans as she wakes from her stupor. The pain in her lower body is the first thing she feels. She is disoriented as the room takes shape around her. It's dark, but a light is burning faintly through the open door. Her head is spinning. Then she becomes aware of the other aches. Everything inside her is aching. Her head, her stomach, her legs. Her body jerks from the cold. She tries sitting up, but the pain in her belly is too severe. She falls back onto the bed.

What has happened? Where am I? She wonders. Where are Barry and Miems? When her eyes get used to the darkness she realises she's not at her brother's house. But where is she? How long has she been sleeping? The pain. The incredible pain in her body. She can't take it. After some time she slowly starts to remember. Yesterday Pieter brought her to this place in the city. Her new place of work. There was a tall guy with blond hair. Anthony. They sat down in a bar and she had a drink. But what happened after that? She shakes her head. Nothing. She can't remember anything else. Her legs feel lame and sticky. She turns on her side and notices a lamp next to the bed. She switches it on. The dim light cast by the 40-watt globe somehow makes the pain more tangible. The cold makes her body tremble. She sits up slowly and looks at her legs, trying to make sense of the stickiness. Her legs are covered in dried blood. She notices she's not wearing her jeans and pan-ties. She also notices how red and swollen she is, how the blood is caked between her legs. She lies back again. Every-thing hurts as much as six years ago, just like that first time with the teacher in the stable. It feels like the lower part of her body is being torn apart.

'Help me! Help!' she screams. She listens. There's no one in the building. She sits up again and puts her feet on the floor. Her shoes are gone. She presses against the walls and furni-ture as she slowly walks out of the room and down the pas-sage to the bar. This is where she was having a drink with the blond guy just now. She turns on every light switch she sees. The clock behind the counter indicates that it's half past two in the morning. The smell of cigarette smoke clings to the inside of the bar. She has to get away from here, and quickly, she thinks, confused. She recalls the way from the bar to the kitchen door, where she entered yesterday. The door is locked. She walks back to the bar and notices the main entrance to the right. It seems to be a reception area with a desk and some plastic flowers in a vase. Next to the vase she notices an open guestbook displaying five columns: date, time, a name, another name and an amount. The front door is also locked and a thick padlock is attached to the security gate on the inside of the door. She shakes the security gate hysterically.

'Help me!' she screams through the door, hoping someone passing outside might hear her. 'Help me! Please, help me! Help me!'

Her screams reverberate through the club. Dejected, she walks back through the reception and bar areas and down the passage. Maybe, just maybe, there is another door somewhere. There are five tiny rooms on the left down the passage, a single bed inside each one. The room with the double bed she woke up in is on the right. Next to it there's a huge bathroom with three showers and two separate toilets. The passage ends at a door with a sign that reads 'PRIVATE'. She turns around and walks back to the kitchen to get some water. She opens the refrigerator. It is stacked with cans of soft drinks and a variety of food: cold meats, sliced cheese, biltong and bowls of salad. She's hungry but can't eat anything. She feels the nausea pushing up her throat just looking at the food, but she takes a bottle of water and chases it down her dry throat. Then she notices her suitcase, still on top of the kitchen cupboard. She takes it and goes to the bathroom. She has to clean herself and put on warm clothes, she thinks to herself. She turns on the hot tap in one of the showers and undresses. Only now does she realise she's not wearing her bra. Purple bruises cover her sixteen-year-old breasts; she notices red bite marks all over her lower body. The blood is clotted brown around her pubic area and down her thighs. The tears come only when the hot water starts to run down her broken body. She slumps to her knees in the corner of the shower as the water washes away the physical remains of the gang rape.

Seven

Engela wakes up when she hears the sound of a door opening. A key rattles in the security gate. After taking a shower a couple of hours earlier she had put on her tracksuit and a jersey. She didn't go back to the room, but fell asleep on the couch in the bar. She can hear the gate being opened and locked again, and then the sound of footsteps in the reception area.

'Hello! Hello!' the man calls out. 'Where are you, little one?'

The man with the blond hair and blue eyes stands in front of her. He takes her hand and pulls her from the couch. Engela peeps down the passage and notices the daylight through the open front door. Cars are going down the street and people are passing on the pavement. But the security gate is locked. Anthony sits her down on a bar-stool. She pulls the jersey over her knees.

'I want to go home, please.' Her words are hardly audible through the sobbing. 'Please, I just want to go home . . .'

Anthony puts his arms around her in an almost fatherly fashion. 'Relax, relax. You are safe here. We'll look after you.

59

You want to make lots of money, I've heard.' He goes behind the bar counter and pours two brandies and Coke. He puts one of the glasses down in front of her.

'Let me go, please, sir. I am in pain. My body is aching badly.'

He grins and takes a sip from the glass. 'Now, now, it's not that bad . . .'

'I was bleeding, sir, I have to get to my sister-in-law. She'll be able to help me.'

'Don't worry, you'll be fine in two days. Drink up.'

'What kind of place is this?'

Anthony looks around the room with a sense of pride. He waves his left arm through the air. 'This, this is a club. Lady Femmé. It's a place attractive women like you can come to for lots of money. And all you have to do is provide the clients with a little bit of pleasure and enjoyment. You understand, don't you?'

Engela shakes her head. 'No, I just want to . . . go home . . . please.'

Anthony gets up, comes around the bar counter and stands behind her. His hands move down her shoulders under her tracksuit top in search of her breasts. She backs away, gets up and sits down on the next bar-stool. He laughs. He puts his hand in his pocket and produces a white pill that he leaves on the bar counter in front of her. 'Swallow that, it'll help for the pain.'

Then he sits down again behind the bar counter. Engela is crying uncontrollably. 'I don't want to! Where is Pieter? Can I please call him to come and get me? Please! Please! I don't want to be here!'

It's eleven on the clock behind the bar. It must be Saturday morning, she thinks. Yesterday was Friday when Pieter dropped her, right? There's a big poster to the left of the clock. The girl in the picture stares at her. Her long, blonde hair is draped in curls over her bare shoulders. Her breasts are big and shiny and wet. She is sitting on a chair with her hand between her legs.

A sour taste pushes up into Engela's throat. 'Can I . . . please have some water?'

Anthony swings around and takes a bottle of water from the bar fridge behind him. 'There.' His patience is wearing thin. 'Take the pill. For the pain.'

She places the pill on her tongue and swallows. The water is cold and comforting. Anthony lights a cigar and leans on his arms on the counter.

'You are . . . what? Standard eight?'

Engela nods her head.

'So, then you're definitely not a virgin. Tell me, how much did you get paid each time you opened your little legs?' His words are cold and emotionless. As if he's asking how many sugars she takes in her coffee. Engela folds her arms tightly in front of her in an attempt to stop her body from shaking. There were times, yes . . . with Marius and his Group 13 when they would fool around as a group. Tongues entering and exiting different mouths. Sweaty bodies rubbing against each other. All for the group and for fun. Before, it was the Saturday afternoons . . . and the vegetables in Mr de Wet's Nissan Skyline when he dropped Barry and her at their house.

She is startled when Anthony brings his hand down on the bar counter. 'How much?' he shouts. 'How much money did you make?'

She shakes her head. 'Nothing . . . nothing . . . but I—'

'Exactly my point. Nothing. But here I am giving you the opportunity to do what you're already doing and make a lot of money at the same time. And what do you do? You sit here crying and whingeing that you want to go home.'

'Please, I don't want to be here. Can I please . . . I just wanted a job . . . why am I being locked up?'

'Do you know what your problem is? You are bloody ungrateful. I offer you the chance of a lifetime. Money. A place to stay. Food. On Monday we'll go buy you the nicest clothes. And you sit whimpering like a dog!'

He gulps down the last of his brandy and Coke and slams the glass on the bar counter. Then he gets up and goes to the kitchen. Engela can hear plastic bags rustling as he unpacks the shopping. The refrigerator door opens and closes. She gets up and goes to the reception hall and jerks the security gate. It's locked. The pavement is deserted. She goes back to the room she woke up in early this morning and curls up on the bed. She doesn't understand why she is shaking so much when it's not cold. She pulls the blanket over her and listens to the man unpacking glasses in the bar. Her shoulders aren't shaking that much and the pain is slowly fading. She just lies there; her thoughts are also separating from her body. In the distance she faintly hears the man's footsteps coming down the passage, and then back again. Doors opening and closing. Then the refrigerator door again. Noise in the kitchen. A bottle jingling. The sound of a soft drink can being opened. The noises are fading around her. The cold and the pain dissolve together. Then she falls asleep.

Don't, mummy, please, she moans through the images chasing her in her dreams. I want to go home . . . I just want to go home . . .

*   *   *

'Go! Get out of my house,' her dad shouts. He loses his balance from all the booze in his body and supports himself against the wall in the lounge. 'You and your whore child! Get lost!'

It's three years earlier, 1990, just after Engela started standard six at Fichardt Park High. She lies in bed, listening to her parents' cheap-wine arguing in the lounge. Usually the pillow she pulls over her head comforts her, but not tonight. You and your whore child, her father's words echo through the house. She? A whore child? Why is he saying that? She hears her mother phoning someone to come pick them up. Then she staggers to the bedroom to pack a suitcase. In between, her parents spit curses at each other.

'You're a no-good piece of rubbish!'

'Fuck off, whore!' her dad retorts.

'I don't want to see you ever, ever again!'

'Suits me. Suits me just fine, you hear me?'

A cupboard door slams. Her father sways back to the lounge and pours another glass of wine.

'I should never have married you, bastard!' her mother's words reel after his footsteps.

'And I also not you, bitch!'

Half an hour later a car stops in front of the house. Engela's mother jerks her from her bed. 'Get dressed,' she demands. 'Tonight we get the hell out of this house.'

They get into the car idling outside. Engela recognises the man behind the steering wheel: he's one of her mother's colleagues, who occasionally picks her up for work in the mornings. Through the car window she stares at her father as he clings to the pillar on the stoep and shakes his arm in anger, but she can't hear what he's saying. The lights on Curie Avenue shine into the car and onto her mother's hand resting on the driver's thigh. They pass the showgrounds and the National Hospital. After twenty minutes they stop in front of the Fountains Inn Hotel in Markgraaff Street and book a room. She gets to sleep on the couch and the grown-ups on the double bed.

Just before the bar closes at midnight the man orders a whisky and lemonade for her mother and himself. She turns her back on them and falls asleep in her tracksuit. She's awake again after a while. She can hear the moaning coming from the double bed. 'Mum?' she asks sleepily. She notices the man's movements on top of her mother.

'Don't, mummy, don't!' she shouts. 'I want to go home!'

'Stop, the child's awake,' Dorothy whispers.

'Shit,' the man pants but doesn't stop.

'Yes, shit,' her mother says and forgets about the woken child on the couch.

Engela gets up and puts her shoes on. She takes her closed suitcase and peeps briefly at the movements on top of the double bed before she moves towards the bedroom door. Slowly she turns the knob and then pulls the door closed behind her. The corridor is empty. Downstairs at reception a man in a hotel uniform sits sleeping. As she steps onto the pavement the tears come. She walks crying down Zastron Street in the direction where Hoffman Square should be. At the Spar in Aliwal Street she finds herself in more familiar surroundings. She crosses the street to the right. There's no traffic.

Half an hour later she sits down on the brightly lit steps of the post office on the eastern side of Hoffman Square. She hates her mother, she thinks. She's a piece of rubbish. After some time she catches her breath and starts walking again. Across the deserted square and down Church Street to the left. She walks and walks. Over the small bridge that takes the road across the dry canal towards Fauna. Now and then a big truck passes her on the way to the N8 interchange outside the city. The trucks slow down when a red light flashes and then continue on.

A car passes, stops and turns around. 'Looking for a lift?'

the driver asks through the open window. Engela ignores him. He's driving slowly next to her. 'Come on, where are you off to?' It sounds like he's slurring. 'Hop in, you pretty thing, hop in.' She walks faster. 'We can have a good time, the two of us. It's cold out here, but I'll warm you up nicely. Nice and warm!'

She feels the swear words forming on her tongue, but she swallows them. She quickens her pace without looking at him.

'Okay then,' says the young man, annoyed. 'If you want to be upstairs, have it your way.'

He speeds off with tyres screeching. Engela walks and walks. Another truck passes. She reckons that it takes about twenty-five minutes to travel by bus from Fauna to the square. On foot, it's probably two to three hours. When again she hears a car coming up from behind, she considers waving her thumb. But she has second thoughts and the car passes. Slowly the night turns to day and the sky changes to orange. Just before the sun appears she knocks on their front door. Once, twice, then for a third time, a little harder. She can hear the key turning, the door handle pushed down and the door opening. Her father is wearing his tattered dressing gown. His hair is untidy from sleep and his eyes are unfocused. He looks at her, she looks at him. Last night she was the whore child who had to leave the house with her mother.

'Dad . . . I want to come back home . . . Dad.'

He starts crying. Later Engela would recall it was the first time ever her father had held her and pressed her against him.

* * *

I want to go home. I just want to go home, she mutters as she tries desperately to escape her nightmare. She jumps up, bewildered, and, like her father on that morning three years earlier, tries to focus as she observes her surroundings. She's not in her bed in Fauna, where her dream had placed her, or in her bedroom in Dewetsdorp or in her brother's flat in Bloemfontein. She's still at Lady Femmé. She listens, but the place is dead quiet. The man with the blond hair who was unpacking the shopping in the kitchen is gone. She gets up. It's five, the bar clock tells her. She jerks the security gate in the reception hall once again, but it remains locked. She lies flat on her stomach and peeps through the narrow gap under the door. It's light outside. It is still day, she thinks. While walking through the bar back to the kitchen she notices more and more pictures of naked girls on the walls. The kitchen door is also locked. She has to get out of here before the guy returns. She becomes frightened. Why is no one looking for her? Why doesn't a police car stop outside and break the door down? She takes a knife and starts chipping at the lock on the wooden kitchen door, but she can't manage to remove it. Then she runs to the front door and forces the knife between the steel gate and the door frame to bend it open. Only the knife bends. She fetches a long breadknife from the kitchen and chips at the wooden door again. Slowly the pain crawls back up her body. She becomes aware of a new stickiness between her legs. She must have started bleeding again while she was asleep. She chips at the wood. A loose splinter pricks her hand. She runs to the bathroom and opens the shower tap. The fresh blood from her hand sticks to it. She rinses her hand and undresses. There's a full-length mirror against the wall. She observes the naked girl in the mirror. Like all the other naked girls on the walls, this one also stares back at her. But this one has wild eyes that want to run away. Engela notices the bruises on the girl's upper legs, arms and back. It looks like she must have fallen down really hard and then tumbled against something.

66

The steam from the hot water hides the girl in the mirror and her image fades away. For a long time Engela stands under the stream of water mixing with the blood and running down the drain. She wishes she could also disappear like that – with the water down the drain. Gone. She was taught in Sunday school class, when she was still in primary school, that the blood of Jesus washes your sins away like water until you're cleansed. She pours a good amount of liquid soap onto her hand from the green bottle in the shower rack. She scrubs and washes her body. More soap, more scrubbing. She wants to wash the bruises away. She wants to wash last night away. She wants to wash Mr de Wet and Group 13 away. Soap, water, wash. Over and over. Then more soap. That night she ran away to Naval Hill three months ago must also be washed away. All the damaged gravestones, all the pages torn from the Bible. Soap and wash. Soap and wash, until the bottle of liquid soap is empty. When you are washed clean you are a new person, the Sunday school teacher said. She wants to be a new person with a new body, Engela thinks. A new body without bruises. But in order to be a clean girl you have to bath every night, wash your hair and look after yourself, the teacher in the health sciences class at school used to say. She has to do all these things, Engela thinks in a haze. Later, much later, the hot water from the shower head becomes lukewarm. Engela opens the hot water tap even more, but the water only gets colder. She steps out of the shower. She's looking for the naked teenage girl in the mirror, but she is hidden in a cloud of steam. She's gone, and Engela wonders if everything has been washed away.

In the kitchen she notices the full refrigerator. She prepares a sandwich of cold meat and cheese spread and wolfs it down. But the sandwich doesn't want to stay inside her. Engela runs to the bathroom and grips the basin as her jerking body rejects every bite of the sandwich.

Two years ago, when her mother moved out, the same thing happened. Her body also jerked. She looks up: the girl in the mirror is back.

Eight

Later that night, in the double bed at the club, Engela's night-mares still haunt her, pushing her down, wrestling with her, pushing her over the bed, pulling the blankets off her. Mr de Wet sits down next to her, strokes her cheek with the palm of his hand, and then moves softly down her neck. She jerks her head to the other side of the bed. His hand glides over her thigh.

'Come, we have to go and feed the horses. And they have to be brushed as well.'

'I don't want to! I don't want to any more! Leave me alone!' she shouts, but the shouting remains in her head. It won't emerge. He pulls her up and holds her hand as they walk through the bar, down the passage and to another room. It's a stable. Satan's head is buried in the feed trough. Engela gets onto the wooden chair to reach the horse's back. She brushes and brushes.

'That's nice,' says Mr de Wet behind her. His hand slides up her dress between her legs to where he pulls at her panties. His hand brushes between her legs. She keeps brushing and brushing Satan's quivering coat. His finger moves up and down when it slides into her. She can hear him panting behind her. Satan neighs and jerks his neck back.

'Remember, he gives us food!' she can hear her brother shouting somewhere outside down the passage.

Mr de Wet picks her up from the chair and puts her down on the ground. He pulls off her panties and with his free hand pushes her dress up over her stomach. It feels as if everything inside her is being torn apart. She can smell the hay and the sweat from the horses. It pushes and wriggles inside her.

'I don't want to! I don't want to any more! I want to go home!'

Only now the screaming escapes her lips. She jumps up in the bed. Her shoulders are shaking. She feels the pain again down in her belly. Mr de Wet and Satan are gone; there is only the bedside lamp next to her. She doesn't know for how long she has slept or what the time is. She picks up the blanket from the floor and pulls it over her. Her head is spinning and she falls back into the pillow.

'Dad . . . I just want to come home . . . Dad,' her lips quiver.

* * *

Dorothy came back home that same evening. Through her bedroom window Engela saw the man dropping her mother at the door. It's the same guy who picked them up the previous night and took them to the hotel. Engela didn't go outside; she hated her mother. Throughout the early hours of the morning, with every step homeward, the hate grew stronger. They never spoke about that night; everybody carried on as if nothing had happened. Her parents were still drinking after work every day. Then they argued. Everything was as always. Nothing had changed.

But things weren't the same when, three months later, Engela returned home from school. She left her bicycle against the stoep, pressed down on the front door handle and entered. The lounge was empty. She saw two plates, two cups and two glasses on the shelf in the kitchen. Nothing else. In her bedroom everything was the same as it was when she had left for school. She left her schoolbag on her bed and went to her parents' bedroom. It was also empty. She opened the wardrobe: all her mother's clothes were gone. Her father's clothes were still on his side. Stunned, Engela sat down on the stoep outside. She realised her mother had left them. She had taken everything and left. Engela remained on the stoep until her father got home, just after five o'clock. She jumped up and shouted: 'Dad, Mum is gone!'

He just nodded. He knew.

'But she didn't say anything, Dad! She just left without saying goodbye.'

Her father was carrying a Pep Stores shopping bag with a new blanket inside. He slept under it on the bedroom floor for the next few days. After a week a social worker came around to take her away, saying it would be better if she stayed with other people for a while.

Your father is not competent to look after you at the moment, the lady in the nice dress and stylish hair said. She smelt of ripe apricots, Engela remembers. The lady would visit her every week. They would sit alone in the lounge and the lady would ask her about her mum and dad and how she felt. But Engela could never lift the lid of her chest of thoughts completely. Frankly, she didn't know how; she had never learnt this skill. She didn't know how to tell the lady, who wore a different dress every week, that she was angry with her mother. Angry because she had just left without saying a word. And angry because, after all those weeks, she hadn't contacted them. She also couldn't talk about the anger she felt when the alcohol made her mom and dad fight in the evenings. Even more so, she couldn't talk about the pain between her legs on those Saturdays out at Mr de Wet's plot. All these things she kept in her chest of thoughts with the lid tight shut.

'Fine, thanks, Miss, the people are looking after me nicely,' Engela said every time. Or: 'How is my dad, Miss?' She never talked about her mother, and did not even ask about her for quite some time.

'He's doing fine,' the lady would say. 'He has stopped drinking and he's finding his feet again.'

After three months the lady from the welfare said she could go back to her dad. Engela realised he was trying his utmost to be a good father to her for the first time. He would cook dinner every night when he got home from work. For the first time in her life she had a lunchbox packed with sandwiches for school. Maybe it was her mother that made him drink all that time, Engela often thought. Just to get away from it all? Sometimes she thought she missed her mother, but why would she? She would kill that thought straight away. But then, after six months and just before Christmas 1990, she couldn't any more. She asked her dad out of the blue one evening if he knew where her mother was. He just shook his head, got up and went to his room. He returned after a while holding a piece of paper.

'There,' he said and pushed the note into her hand. 'Your mother's phone number. She's living in the city in a flat somewhere. Call her if you like.'

Engela carried the piece of paper with her for a week. What if her mother didn't want to speak to her? To have nothing to do with her? But when she dialled the number that Friday night her mother gave her the address immediately and invited her to come visit the very next day. Engela took the bus to the square and then walked to the address written on the piece of paper. She arrived in the lobby of the block of flats half an hour before their agreed time. She wasn't sure what to do. The lift doors opened and a tall, thin man stepped out. He was wearing a South African Airways uniform. When he noticed her, he stopped and stared. He didn't say anything, just looked at her, turned and disappeared on the pavement outside. Engela wasn't sure why she felt so uncomfortable at that particular moment.

That morning they didn't talk about what had happened over the last few months or why her mother didn't contact her and her father. They just chatted and told silly jokes, and that was all Engela wanted. For a change her mother was well looked after; she drank only fruit juice and the flat was nice and clean. Maybe her parents were just not meant for each other, she thought. Maybe they were not good for each other and brought out the worst in each other.

When they said their goodbyes after three hours, Dorothy asked if she had seen the man in the pilot's uniform when she arrived. Yes, Engela answered. Her mother smiled. It was a sweet smile of someone in love. Like someone bumping into her first love after many years. That was how her mother smiled that day.

A month later – also a Friday night, the first Friday of January 1991 – her father didn't cook for the first time since the previous August. It was also the first time that he again came home from work with a yellow Solly Kramer's bag. He sat outside on the stoep all evening. From her bedroom she listened to the sounds coming from outside: her dad sobbing, the opening and closing of the screw top of the brandy bottle, her dad crying. He only came inside after ten. His uneven footsteps as he staggered down the passage ended in a thud on his bed. Engela got up and went to the kitchen to prepare her dinner: a can of baked beans on two slices of bread.

The news that her mother was getting married again and would move to Dewetsdorp made him stop at Solly Kramer's every afternoon after that. Self-medication. All of a sudden the father Engela had got to know the previous year – the one who cared and provided – wasn't there. All that remained of him was an empty shell sitting on the stoep every night, opening and closing a brandy bottle. For that reason, Engela moved in with her mother in Dewetsdorp in March. Later she would write in her diary:

> Unfortunately I discovered that my stepfather was very jealous and got aggressive when he drank. And so the arguing started again.

* * *

The images from her past keep attacking her: there are knives, a pistol, screams, blood. An ugly man stares at her every so often. He wants to come and take her away. 'You are mine, you gave yourself to me,' he repeats, over and over, with a grin. 'Remember Naval Hill? Remember the cemetery in Dewetsdorp? There is absolutely no chance of turning back now. That's why you are here. You are mine and I can do with you what I like.'

He straddles her and clasps his hands around her throat. 'You are mine! Get it? Mine only!' He presses her tightly against the pillow and dribbles over her face. There's fire in his eyes. His breath is here, right here in her face. It smells like a decapitated cat that's been lying on a grave, rotting in the sun all week.

'Get off! Get off me!' Engela yells and jerks from side to side. Somebody else is pressing her mouth shut. It's Mr de Wet. He pushes and pushes into her before disappearing. To her left her father is lying on the floor of the lounge. He gurgles as he struggles to breathe. Her mother is sitting on top of him, the knife against his throat. 'Today I'm going to kill you, arsehole!'

The grinning man is wearing a black cape. He's standing in the corner of the room and observes the game with amusement. Suddenly another man appears, her stepdad. He is holding a pistol. He presses it against her mother's head. Engela notices a Bible on the side table next to her. She grabs it and tears the pages out one by one. She crumples the pages and throws them into the air. They catch fire. The smell of sulphur hangs in the air. The man in the black cape stands in the corner and smiles with satisfaction. He is standing in a pool of blood. The blood streams over her mother's double bed in Dewetsdorp. It splatters across the images that overlap in slow motion.

'I can do with you what I like,' the man in the cape shouts in ecstasy.

Engela wants to scream, but Mr de Wet is back to press her mouth shut. 'Shut up! I'm coming! I'm coming!'

Engela can hear a shot ring out. Blood gushes from her mother's mouth and ears and spatters over Engela's body. The blood is warm and wet. I just want to go home, please, I just want to go home, Engela cries. But no one can hear her above all the noise . . .

Her body is soaked in sweat when she wakes up. She goes to the toilet first, and then to the kitchen. Engela has no sense of time. Whatever the clock shows means nothing to her. Is it day or night? Sometimes she peeps under the front door to see if the sun is out. But what day is it? Saturday, Sunday, Monday?

Or maybe it's the next weekend already. How many days has she been locked up? She doesn't know. The border between night and day doesn't exist. Everything is just a grey whole. The hours between being awake and sleeping, between reality and the nightmares, between thinking and remembering, are so interlaced she can no longer tell them apart. Is she dreaming? Is she awake? She doesn't know. She takes the last white pill Anthony left in the bar for her. It will help for the pain, he had said. When was that again? Yesterday, the day before yesterday, last week? She downs the pill with a double brandy and Coke. Sometimes she takes food from the refrigerator. Sometimes she stands under the shower until the water runs cold. Then she gets back into bed. She dreams the police arrive with tyres screeching, kick open the door and save her.

*   *   *

Engela can hear a key turning in the kitchen door. It opens with a crunch. Then another key in the padlock of the security gate. The chain rattles. The voices of two women become audible. Is she awake or not? She doesn't know. A man is talking to them. She recognises the voice. It's Anthony's. Engela sits up. The man with the devilish smile and the black cape is gone. Somebody came and cleaned up the blood, she notices.

The voices in the bar are laughing. 'Hello Monday, hello new week, we are back!' one of the women says. Lights are switched on and more light streams into the room. The voices approach the room. A woman walks into the room and turns on the ceiling light first. Engela shields her eyes with her hand.

'Still asleep?' the woman asks. She sits down on the bed next to Engela. 'Come on. Time to get up. It's four o'clock already. We have to get ready for tonight.'

The woman hugs her. 'Hi, I'm Jacky. Don't worry, you'll be okay.'

'Hi, I'm Nadia,' the other one waves.

Engela stares with sleepy eyes at the two women in the room. They're both young, definitely younger than thirty, it seems. She notices Jacky's blonde beauty at once. Nadia's hair is in a bob and she's as pretty, but her figure is more like the softness of a mother.

'Don't be afraid, Engela, we're here to look after you,' Nadia says. Consoling, like a mother. 'You just have to do what we do. We'll teach you. Everything will be fine, you'll see. But you have to go take a shower first.'

'Yes, and then we'll make you pretty,' Jacky says.

'I don't want to. Please, I just want to go home,' Engela pleads and swallows at the tears welling up in her throat. 'Please, call the police to come and get me. Or just let me go, please.'

'It's not that bad, Engela,' Nadia says. 'You'll be making lots of money here. Your whole life is waiting.'

'What . . . what do I have to do?'

'Don't worry. I told you we'll teach you everything you need to know.'

'And we will look after you. You don't have to be afraid. We'll see to it that nothing happens to you. But you are going to have to take a shower first.'

On the way to the bathroom Engela can hear them laugh and talk. This time she doesn't wait for the water to go cold; she showers quickly and puts on her tracksuit again. Back in the room Nadia is sitting in front of the mirror, make-up brush in one hand. She is dressed in underwear only.

'That's for you,' Jacky says behind her. 'We want you to be okay.'

Engela takes the glass. Brandy, thank goodness, she sighs.

'And this is a tranquilliser. Just to make you feel better.' Engela swallows the white pill.

'Let's start with your hair,' Nadia says when she puts down her make-up brush. 'Come sit down here by the mirror.'

'And Anthony bought you the most beautiful clothes today,' Jacky says. The two women giggle with excitement. Engela giggles softly. She's not afraid any more. She's happy that Jacky and Nadia are here, even if she doesn't really know them. But they are nice and will look after her. Nadia combs her wet hair. Then she blow-dries it and makes short curls.

'Wow, you have really nice hair,' Nadia says. 'You know, I have always wanted a younger sister whose hair I could do.'

'And here you have her, your own little sister!' Jacky laughs.

Engela also laughs. Her head is spinning a little, probably from the brandy she downed too fast.

'How do you feel,?' Nadia wants to know. The hairdryer blows warmly on her neck.

Engela giggles. 'Nice. It feels like the ground underneath me is floating, but it's pleasant. I feel calm now, thank you. It's nice . . . it's nice . . . to have you here.'

'Excellent,' Jacky says. 'Undress so I can do your make-up.'

Engela chucks her tracksuit in the corner of the room and sits down naked on the dressing table chair. She's not shy any more. Jacky applies a heavy layer of base to her face to hide her teenage skin. Without saying anything, she also applies base to the bruises on Engela's breasts and thighs.

'I would give anything to have a cute body like yours again,' Nadia says. They all giggle. Engela can hear the front door opening in the distance as someone enters. Male voices are coming from the bar. Music starts playing.

'You have to wear this,' Jacky says.

Engela stares reluctantly at the two pieces of clothing Jacky is waving in the air triumphantly. Then the two women help her get dressed. Nadia fastens at the back the tiny top that has to cover her breasts and Jacky pulls the matching miniskirt over her hips.

'Now the shoes. Shoes are very important. Have a look at these. Aren't they beautiful?'

Engela slips on the black high heels, but struggles to keep her balance when she stands up. They burst into laughter at her childish clumsiness. Engela also laughs. She feels wonderful, as she will later describe the moment in her diary.

'You look amazing!' Jacky says.

'Beautiful!' Engela hears Anthony's voice. He is standing in the door and nodding his head approvingly. 'Absolutely beautiful.' He clasps his hands in satisfaction. Two other men appear behind him. 'Boys, meet Sammy-Jo, our new starlet!' He gestures theatrically. They greet her with a nod and then disappear with Anthony.

'They've gone into his office,' Nadia says to Jacky. 'Wonder what's up?'

'Who's Sammy-Jo?' Engela wants to know.

The two older women look at each other. Then they burst out laughing again.

'It's you, sweetie,' Nadia says. 'It's your professional name. From now on you are Sammy-Jo, okay?'

No, Engela shakes her head. She doesn't understand.

'It's like . . .' Nadia tries to explain, but doesn't get any further.

'Remember that hit song from two years ago, "Sacrifice"?' Jacky takes over.

Engela nods. Of course she knows it. Teenagers know all the hits.

'Who sings that song?'

'Simple question,' Engela answers. 'Elton John. Everybody knows that.'

'But do you know his real name?'

'Huh?' Engela doesn't understand.

'Well, everyone knows him as Elton John, but that is only his stage name. His real name is Reginald Dwight.'

'Why?'

'It's what many entertainers do. Like singers or actors. They change their names for their jobs. And here we are also entertainers. That is why we all have professional names. And that is why you are now Sammy-Jo. It's your working name.'

'Okay, I see.'

Engela doesn't really understand why she has suddenly become Sammy-Jo, but she doesn't feel like talking about it. 'Who were those two other guys with Anthony?' she asks.

'The three of them are the club's partners. Anthony is the big boss. The other two are his brothers. The big one who looks like a bodybuilder is George. You'll find him behind the bar counter mostly. He's the nicest of the three, actually. The oldest one is Steve. He's an arsehole, just like Anthony. Later tonight you will meet Jacques. He's not a partner, he only works here. He's a student, cute guy. He always sits at the door, answers the phone, takes the bookings and lets the guests come and go, that kind of stuff.'

'Are those also not their real names?'

The women giggle.

'We're going to have a good time working together, you'll see,' Nadia says. 'We like you. Anyway, enough titivating, we have to go to the front. Come.'

The two older girls take the lead, swinging their hips professionally as they strut down the passage. Engela follows unsteadily on her high heels. She has never worn so little clothing in a public place, but at this stage it doesn't bother her much. They sit down at the corner of the bar and Nadia shows her how to cross her legs.

'You sit like that all night. Crossed legs. Otherwise the men will see your beaver and that's for much later, when we go to the rooms.'

Jacky lights up two cigarettes and gives one to Nadia. George pours a glass of wine for each of them.

'Can't I rather have a brandy . . .' Engela wants to ask.

'No, Sammy-Jo, no!' Jacky reprimands her. 'Ladies don't drink hard liquor in public. Only wine. It's more ladylike. We leave the heavy stuff for when we're alone, okay?'

Engela takes a sip of the wine and recalls the night she and Miems got so drunk on the Tassenberg. When was that again? Last week, the week before? She can't remember. She misses Miems. Why hasn't Miems come looking for her, she wonders. A young man enters from the kitchen and walks up to them. He puts his hand out to Engela.

'Hi, Sammy-Jo, I'm Jacques. Welcome,' he says. I work at the door, or in the kitchen. If you need anything . . . well, just say so.'

He starts chatting to the other two. Engela stares past the bar counter to the lobby. The front door is open; it's just the security gate that's closed. Maybe the gate isn't locked, she thinks. She gets up slowly, the wine glass in her hand, and walks towards the entrance. It's dark outside. The street is busy. Cars are passing. Just two more paces and she'll be at the gate . . . maybe it isn't locked . . .

She feels a strong hand on her shoulder. She turns around. It's the big guy, George. He shakes his head. 'No, Sammy-Jo, you're not allowed this side.' He takes her by the arm and steers her back to the bar counter. 'You stay with Nadia and Jacky all the time.'

Engela crosses her legs again as she sits down. George goes behind the bar and tops up her wine glass.

'See, the nicest thing about this job is the free food and booze,' he laughs.

She laughs back. Jacques disappears into the kitchen, and later she sees him walking to the lobby.

'It's eight already and no one's here yet,' Nadia complains.

'Typical Monday night,' Jacky responds. 'But Jacques says two guys called to say they're coming over at nine.'

'Two? Only two? Bloody hell, what a waste of time.'

Jacques comes back. There's been another booking, he announces. 'A group of six businessmen. They are just finishing up a seminar and then they'll be here. Around ten.'

'Are you ready? For six guys?' he wants to know. He looks at Engela; she looks pretty young in the twilight. Why would she want to work here?

Nadia looks at Jacky, who nods. 'Yes, shit, let them come.'

'The week has kicked off nicely after all!' Nadia calls out.

* * *

Early the next morning Engela wakes up in the double bed. She's naked, she forgot to put her night things on, she notices.

The tiny top and miniskirt she wore last night are draped over the black high-heel shoes. Her head feels thick. The wine she drank last night is making her temples throb. Her bladder feels uncomfortably full. She pulls on a T-shirt and goes to the bathroom. In the small rooms on the left-hand side of the passage she notices Nadia and Jacky fast asleep on the single beds. She goes to the toilet and then washes her hands and face. Then back to the bar where by now she knows the headache tablets are kept. She jerks at the kitchen door and the gate at reception once again. Locked. She takes her diary from her suitcase, gets back into bed and starts writing:

Tuesday, 19 October 1993

There were a lot of men here last night. Eight of them. They are referred to as clients. They were in suits and ties. The owner sort of pushed me into one of the bar's corners. I could hear the two girls chatting to the men. After a while Nadia fetched me and we went to the little rooms at the back. One of the clients came along. In the tiny room with the single bed she made me stand in a corner. I couldn't watch, because what was happening in front of me was too much for me. I just had to wake from the nightmare. She and this guy got undressed and did terrible things to each other. In the room next door I could hear Jacky laughing and making funny noises. I could hear the man with her as well. When they were done Nadia came over to me and whispered in my ear: 'Remember what you saw, that's the way to do it.'

I simply had to watch what they did. From one room to the next I had to go and see what they were doing. It went on for hours. I felt nothing, no pain, no fear, I couldn't cry, I couldn't even speak.

Eventually everything was over, the music had died, the door was locked and everybody was gone, except for the girls and me. We sat down at the bar and they celebrated their innings for the night. They counted their money in front of me and were so excited about how much they had made. But I was like a zombie, just staring ahead of me. The girls promised me that soon I would also have a lot of money and that I could then start a new life.

They told me they were from Johannesburg and that they only worked in Bloemfontein five nights a week. They came in on Monday nights and Fridays nights they would go back home. Their income, or cut, was 50%. The agency got half and they got half. They told me about their fancy houses, their expensive furniture and expensive cars, and how nice their lives were. They didn't have other jobs, they only did this, and Jacky is married with children. Her husband didn't care, as long as the money was good he was happy.

Not one of them wanted to know where I was from, if I have family or anything else about me. I also never asked them their real names. It didn't bother me and meant nothing to me.

* * *

'We're going back home tonight, Sammy-Jo, but you'll be okay,' Jacky says to Engela four evenings later at the bar. The clients are already gone. There's only Jacques in the lobby waiting for the taxi that will take the two girls to the bus terminal. From there they'll travel back to Johannesburg. Engela starts crying and Nadia pours them another double brandy. They've had enough of the wine they have to drink in front of the clients.

'But then I'm going to be all alone again.'

'Only until Monday night, then we'll be back,' Jacky comforts her.

Nadia puts her arm around Engela's bare shoulders. 'You did very well this week, darling. Very well. I think from next week Anthony will let you have your own clients, then it's the big-time money. You'll see.'

Geez, is money all you ever think of? flashes through Engela's head. 'But what about me? It's crap being all by myself. Locked up. It's really crap. Why don't you get that?'

Jacky consoles her: 'Enjoy the break. Sleep and relax. Watch TV. Next week will be long hours again. And take from the bar and the kitchen what you want. Anthony and the gang look after us very well. There's three tranquillisers. Take one a day until we get back. It's from Anthony. On the house. And this stuff is bloody expensive, I'll have you know.'

Engela is thankful for the pills; she's been getting used to them this past week. They make her feel good. She wrote in her diary that they're her forget-pills, her coping pills. But how will she cope the entire weekend without Nadia and Jacky? The tears of sorrow come with the last gulp from her glass.

'You are pretty, Jacky, so pretty. You look like a doll, so pretty. Your skin . . . your big blue eyes, you look like a porcelain doll . . .'

'You too, Sammy-Jo, you too,' Jacky says consolingly as Engela clings to her. The wine they've drunk makes them cry easily.

'Taxi's here,' Jacques shouts.

'See you Monday,' Nadia says.

Engela stays behind in the twilight of the bar. Jacques locks the front door and the gate and sits down behind the bar. 'Gosh, it's been a long week,' he says, as if not expecting a response. 'Seems you have had one too many, but I can fill up your glass if you like.'

She nods. He's wearing a pair of jeans, a two-tone long-sleeve shirt and loafers. He was here every night this past week – between the reception and the kitchen – but they never really spoke.

Monday night before the first clients arrived, the three partners' orders were clear: you don't tell anyone who you are or where you come from, or how old you are. If anyone asks, you say 'twenty-one'. You stay with Nadia and Jacky all the time and don't mingle with clients on your own. They are watching her, she was warned. George is at the bar most of the time.

'I don't really drink, but right now I feel like a beer,' Jacques says. He pours her a single brandy with ice and Coke and takes an ice-cold Castle for himself. He pours the beer into a long glass. The white foam almost runs over the edge of the glass.

'Sammy-Jo, I was going to ask you . . . sorry if it sounds too personal . . . but . . . how old are you?'

It tastes like he has cheated her with this round; it's like Coke without the brandy.

'Twenty-one,' she replies without thinking after a few sips. 'Twenty-one.'

He nods. 'I see.' He finishes his beer in five minutes. 'Then I'm off. See you Monday.'

The back gate opens and closes. He locks it, and then locks the door at the gate. Suddenly the club is quiet. Dead quiet. 'Shit!' Engela shouts and slams the glass down on the bar counter.

Nine

That evening Engela and Barry went to their bedrooms early, as they could sense their parents having another round of arguing.

In the lounge the pitch of their voices increased as the level in the Mainstay bottle dropped.

Barry finished school two years ago but is still staying at home. Well, he sleeps here on occasion. He is sometimes gone for days, but when he turns up unannounced, like tonight, no one asks where he has been. Everyone accepts that he stays with friends. He's had the habit since his school days. After matriculating in 1988 he started working as a mechanic in the city, and after that they started seeing less and less of him. Recently he hinted to Engela that he had a girlfriend and that sometimes he would stay over at her place, rather than with his friend Pieter from work. Her name is Miems.

'And why haven't you come and introduced her to us?' Engela wants to know, with a hint of sarcasm.

Barry was annoyed. 'Do you bring your friends home?'

'Oh, don't be silly.'

Neither of them ever did; they were too embarrassed. By the poverty, the empty refrigerator, their parents' fighting. Engela didn't have friends, in any case.

'You know what, Barry? I can't wait to get out of the house, like you. I also want a job and my own flat that I can decorate and where it would be nice to stay.'

'And what kind of work do you want to do?'

'I don't know . . . any work . . . anything to just get away from here.'

On her second day at Fichardt Park High earlier in the year, her standard six teacher asked Engela to stay after school. She was concerned about her, the teacher had said, without mentioning the contents of her primary school report. And if she wanted to talk, about anything, she should know that her teacher's door was always open. Engela nodded without saying anything. What would be the point, she thought. And anyway, she's not that good at talking. Especially not about the things going down at home . . .

Earlier in the evening Dorothy had cooked cabbage and lemon squash again for dinner and opened two tins of sweet-corn. She and Andries started sniping at each other at the dinner table. That's why Engela and Barry went to their bed-rooms after dinner. Engela finished her homework and Barry paged through the latest edition of *Car* magazine before he turned the light off.

They can hear their parents' voices above the television every now and then. Engela pulls the pillow over her head, the way she does whenever there is a fight. She can hear the wind starting to blow outside. Through the drawn curtains she sees lightning in the distance. Her parents' voices are rising in the lounge. Then she falls asleep.

It is just after midnight when a loud bang wakes her. A flash of lightning illuminates her room through the curtains. Outside the window it thunders and rattles. Suddenly there are other strange noises in the house: gurgling, groaning. She can hear her mother's voice through it all, but it has a different tone. It's not the usual shrill sound; it has a slow, dark undertone. Engela gets out of her bed and walks cautiously down the passage towards the noise. The lightning is dancing all over the place. She notices Barry's bedroom door is closed. The rain is pounding on the zinc roof. The gurgling sound intensifies the closer she gets to the lounge. It sounds like her dad. Another flash outside. The passage is illuminated for two seconds, and then it's dark again. Engela is scared. From the top of the passage a faint ray of light extends from the lounge. Then she's there. Her father is lying on his back on the floor. His face is blue and he is struggling to breathe. He groans and gurgles. He just lies there and doesn't resist her mother, who straddles him. Dorothy's left hand clasps his throat tightly, preventing him from breathing. With her right hand she presses the breadknife against his throat. Tonight she wants to be absolutely certain.

'Mum! Mum!' Engela screams. 'Stop it!'

Engela runs over and tries to release Dorothy's grip on her dad's throat. Dorothy pushes Engela away with her left hand. 'Go back! Go back to your room! Tonight I kill this arsehole!'

The sound of thunder cracks through the lounge and makes the windows rattle. Engela staggers to the floor but is up again in seconds. She grabs her mother. 'Leave him, Mum!' she cries hysterically.

Dorothy slashes at Engela with the knife, grazing her arm. Blood trickles from the wound but Engela hardly notices. She sees her brother storm into the lounge and grab her mother around the waist. He pulls her from the man lying on the floor.

She falls against the coffee table and rolls over, but then she's back on her feet again.

Barry's face glows with anger; Engela has never seen him like this. Dorothy lifts the knife and hurls herself at Barry. A deep, raw, animal-like sound escapes from her throat. She is ready to stab. And then Barry hits her. His fist strikes his mother on her cheek. She staggers backward, bumps into the lamp in the corner and falls over the couch. The light bulb shatters. Outside the raindrops splash against the window. Andries struggles to get up. Blood is running from his mouth. Lightning bolts crack one after the other and illuminate the scene enacted in front of Engela. Red marks that later would turn to blue have already appeared around Andries's throat. He staggers to the bathroom. Dorothy is also unsteady on her feet. The hate flashes from her eyes. 'Get the fuck out of here!' she screams at Barry. 'You will never set foot in this house again!'

Dorothy was right. Barry never did.

*   *   *

As always, they never talked about that night.

'I don't really talk much, miss,' Engela told her teacher. She was too shy to speak. 'But everything is fine, miss, thank you.'

Dorothy moved out and into the flat in Bloemfontein in May. The lady from the welfare said Engela had to go stay with other people who would take care of her for a while, but that she could move back in August. The months after that were the best of her life, Engela thought. Sometime during this time she wrote in her diary:

> No one is fighting in our home. My dad stopped drinking
> and there is money for food. He cooks every night for the

two of us. I can see he is trying his best to make up for everything. There is money for food, for soap and the power isn't cut any more. My parents are divorced now, but I think they still have some contact.

It was only the next January that her father began to stop off at Solly Kramer's again, after they had heard about Dorothy's new boyfriend and that she would be moving to Dewetsdorp. Apparently an old flame had been revived and consolidated. Suddenly the father Engela had got to know since last August – the one who cared and provided – wasn't there. All that remained of his soul was an empty shell that sat and cried on the stoep in the evenings, accompanied by the sound of the bottle cap opening and closing.

That is why Engela went to live with her mother in Dewetsdorp.

On the first day of the winter school holidays in June 1991 she wrote in her diary:

> Wow, amazing things have happened the past three months! I have left Bloemfontein and my mother has put me in a new school and a new life has begun. My mum has everything: a beautiful home, nice furniture, nice clothes and nice shoes. She decorated my bedroom with pretty curtains and a bed set. My mum got married to my stepdad and I was the bridesmaid. It wasn't a big wedding, just some friends came over for a visit. I am much closer to my mum now and I have got to know her for who she really is. I have realised that alcohol can change a person completely, it turns you into a different person.
>
> I have also met this guy. His name is Marius and he is in matric. He's cool. After school I sometimes go to his house.

We listen to his music. He has a lot of records, heavy metal. Cool music. He smokes and drinks beer after school, but I don't do that. He always laughs at me and says one day I will, but I won't. Marius draws these signs in his books and in his school bag. Upside down crucifixes, that kind of thing. He says it makes him feel good. Now I'm also doing it. He was right, it makes one feel good. Marius says he likes me because I'm a rebel and wild and so tough that everyone's apprehensive of me. But deep down I'm actually a timid girl looking for love and help. I don't know why I'm always so cocky, pushing people away. Anyway, tomorrow I'm off to Bloemfontein to visit my dad during the school holidays.

* * *

'Engela, bring the salt!' Dorothy calls out as her daughter goes to the kitchen. Dorothy and Joshua are sitting outside at the fire for the braai. They are dressed warmly; in the southeastern Free State the evenings get bitterly cold, especially in July. That is why they are drinking Old Brown Sherry. The first two-litre bottle is nearly empty.

The winter school holidays have been over for two weeks, but her mother hasn't asked Engela about her dad since her return from Bloemfontein. Engela prefers it that way. When she returns with the salt she can hear her mother and stepfather arguing about something.

'Just leave it,' Joshua grunts. 'You are starting again with your bloody moaning.'

He takes the salt and sprinkles it over the meat.

'When will the meat be ready?' Dorothy asks and tops up her glass. Engela notices how the sherry is already making her mother slur her words.

'When it's ready,' Joshua says bluntly.

'I told you to add more firewood, the meat would have been ready by now, but no . . .'

Joshua becomes annoyed and spins around. He holds the tongs under her nose. 'Who's the bloody man in this house? Hey? Who?'

And with that they pour the last bit of sherry. Engela goes to her room; tonight she doesn't feel like listening to their arguing. Her mother calls her after thirty minutes to come and eat. They eat outside at the fire, because that's the way Joshua wants it. A braai isn't a braai when it's dished up and served inside, he always says. They eat in silence. She has to be thankful for everything Joshua is doing for them, Engela thinks. Even though he has a temper and dictates, and is jealous of her mother.

'Thanks for the food, it was good,' Joshua says sarcastically when they're all done.

Engela observes the tiny clouds of vapour escaping and then dissolving as she breathes. Sometimes she wishes she could also disappear like that. Dorothy ignores her husband's comment.

'Is the bottle empty?' she wants to know.

'What does it look like? What do you think?' he hits back.

'Engela, bring another one, please. It's in the cupboard in the passage.'

'Mum!' Engela pleads. 'Hasn't it been enough?'

Dorothy is annoyed. 'Don't talk back! I told you to bring the other bottle of sherry!'

'Yes, lately you have become too big for your boots,' Joshua adds his opinion.

Engela gets up slowly. She's scared, but she fetches the bottle and goes back to her bedroom. Even with the door closed she can hear her mother and stepfather arguing outside. Later he storms into the house, swearing, and goes to the main bedroom. A cupboard door is opened and shut with a bang. Again the swearing as he returns down the passage.

'Fucking bitch!' Joshua shouts on his way out.

Engela wants to pull the pillow over her head when she hears her mother scream.

'No, Joshua, no!'

'Tonight you die!'

'Stop it, please, stop it!' Dorothy pleads.

Engela runs outside. Joshua is gripping her mother's head from behind. With his pistol against her temple he shouts: 'I will shoot you, you hear me!'

Dorothy is crying. 'Please, Joshua, please, don't . . .'

'Uncle Joshua! Leave my mother alone!' Engela shouts from the kitchen door.

'Uncle Joshua!'

'Say goodbye to your mother. Tonight's her last fucking night on this earth!' Joshua doesn't move. He looks at Engela, and then at Dorothy.

'Go back to your room!'

'Don't, Uncle Joshua! I'll call the neighbours. I'll call the police!'

'Your mother is driving me crazy, you hear me? Crazy!'

'Joshua—'

'Shut up, bitch!' He presses harder with the pistol.

Engela doesn't know what to do. She just stands there in the kitchen door, crying. Her mother, who always used to threaten her father, has become the victim. She descends the steps and wants to get closer, to stop him, but he points the pistol in her direction.

'Stay where you are! Stay where you are or I'll blow you to pieces!'

She freezes.

'Do you know what your problem is?' he demands from Dorothy and Engela. 'You two don't listen to me.'

'Uncle?'

'Joshua, calm down.'

'Shut up, shut up!'

Engela wants to turn and run. Through the house and out the front door. Across the street. Help! Help! she wants to shout. But suddenly the back yard goes quiet. No one says a word. Joshua looks at Engela, then at the pistol in his hand. He pushes Dorothy aside, shoves the pistol into his pocket and storms into the house. Engela can hear him slam the bedroom door. Her mother gets up from where she fell against the braai. A thin line of blood trickles down her forehead. She walks slowly towards the house, where Engela stands outside the kitchen door, her hands clasped over her mouth. The sherry she's drunk makes her stumble.

'My child. My dear child,' Dorothy cries as she embraces Engela.

'Let's run away, Mum. Let's run away really far,' the fourteen-year-old pleads while sobbing.

But they didn't. He is a good man, he looks after us, Dorothy explained. Just before Engela fell asleep that night, she thought: I flipping hate him.

Ten

When Engela wakes up the next morning she notices an empty bottle on the dressing table with a note attached: 'Urinate in the bottle and leave it on the kitchen cupboard.' Her allowance of two white pills is next to the bottle. She doesn't understand the point of the note, but she's too tired to worry about it. She's too tired to cry. She is exhausted – her soul, her body, her everything. Everything is exhausted. She stumbles to the bathroom. On the way back she leaves the bottle on the kitchen cupboard as instructed. She get back into bed. She wants to cry, but she's too tired for that too. She swallows one of the pills. She knows it will make her feel better. Then she starts to pray, for the first time in three years. She begs for a miracle, that she will touch the front door and it will open. She asks Him nicely because she believes it will happen. After a few moments she gets up again and walks to the front door. She yanks at the door, but it's still locked. Locked. Furious, she jerks the door once more. 'God! You don't exist! You don't exist!' she yells. 'I asked You nicely, very nicely, but You don't help me!' She rattles the door hysterically. It remains locked. 'You don't exist! Where are You when I need you? Where are You? Why don't You open the door? Why not!' She staggers back to the bedroom, yelling. 'Why don't You open the door! Why not! Why not!' She falls down on the bed. 'Marius was right all the time. You don't exist. It's your fault I'm here! It's all your fault!'

As the pill enters her bloodstream and reaches her brain, through the sobs the pain and the anger dissolve. She is gliding on a cloud to another dimension. To a place where there is no pain or anger, where there's no remembering. It's fantastic, she thinks, before the illusions take her off to dreamland. She finds herself in a big park with many trees. A notice with her picture is nailed to every tree. The notice says in big, bold letters: 'LOST'. Groups of people gather around the trees to read the notice. She stands in front of them and waves her arms. 'I'm here!' she shouts. 'I'm here!'

But nobody sees her . . .

*   *   *

'Bloodbath in Paradise,' the thirteen teenagers sing and scream to Ozzy Osbourne. Marius du Preez takes the next album, Cheap Trick's *Dream Police*, from 1979, from his record collection. He lowers the stylus onto track four. 'Gonna Raise Hell'. This track plays for just over nine minutes.

'And what are your plans for the holidays?' Susan had inquired of her stepdaughter two days before the start of the July holidays of 1993. They were doing the dishes. Ever since she married Andries, three months ago, Susan has tried her best to befriend the sixteen-year-old Engela, but Engela's not an easy one. A rebel, Susan told Andries despondently.

'Not much,' Engela responded. She wipes the dishes with the cloth. 'But this Saturday I'm going to watch a video at a friend's place. Girly stuff, you know.'

Engela is an expert liar; she uses the name of a fictitious friend because she knows her stepmother doesn't know the children from school or the people in town. What she can't mention at all is the fact that she and the rest of the Group 13 gang will be having a garage party at Marius' house. His parents are away again for the weekend and they will have the house all to themselves, he said when he invited them a week ago.

By ten o'clock that evening Grim Reaper's 'Final Scream' is next on Marius' playlist; Queen follows with 'Another One Bites the Dust'.

The garage is dimly lit with 13 black deco candles burning on the tool shelves against the walls. A gas heater hisses in a corner. It's winter outside, but in here the party is warming everyone up. Out there life is gloomy, but in here the balm of alcohol soothes their bodies. Tongues meet eagerly in the half light; hands in search of love slide over breasts and erections while Judas Priest sing 'Better By You, Better Than Me'. The music stops. Everyone looks at Marius standing in front of the hi-fi. He lifts his hand to indicate they should be quiet. He wants to say something. 'Get stoned and worship Satan!' he yells.

'Get stoned and worship Satan,' they all yell back. They know what his next treat is going to be. He puts down next to the hi-fi the green Tupperware container filled with the best dagga from Lesotho. As always, when Marius's parents go away they leave him plenty of money to compensate for their absence.

'Potent stuff, this,' Marius says. He got it earlier that day from his connection just outside of town. The party becomes more relaxed. Uriah Heep plays softly in the background. The group sit cross-legged, rolling the dagga into joints. Soon the bittersweet fumes fill the air around the thirteen teenagers and the thirteen candles.

'We are thirteen, but actually we are one,' Marius philosophises. He stares at the opposite corner of the garage. 'Nobody knows about us, nobody knows we're here, only we do.'

Everybody nods in agreement. Yes, only they know. They are one.

Marius knocks the ashes carefully into an empty KOO tin placed on the floor in the centre of the circle, and puts the lit joint down next to it. Then, opening the blade of his pocket knife, he makes a cut on the inside of his arm and stares in ecstasy at the blood trickling slowly from the skin. He passes the knife to the teenager sitting to the left of him so he can also cut himself. Another trickle of blood appears on the inside of an arm. The bloodstained knife is passed around the group of teenagers until it reaches Engela, who is last to drive the blade through her skin. They turn to each other and mix their blood by smearing it onto each other's wounds.

'We are one,' Marius muses again. He gets up, goes to the hi-fi and stack of records on top of the workbench and chooses an album that was released in 1991. The cover art shows a naked baby boy swimming under water in a blue swimming pool, his arms outstretched, towards a dollar note dangling from a fishing hook in front of him. Marius lowers the needle onto Nirvana's big hit, 'Smells Like Teen Spirit'. The seated teenagers sway to and fro. Now and then a glowing cigarette end finds the KOO tin in the centre of the circle.

'Dudes, tonight I have some big news,' Marius says slowly. He waits for everyone's empty eyes to fix on him before he continues, deliberately. 'The climax of the Satanists' calendar is coming up in two months' time. In October. Already small groups are getting together in preparation for the big day . . . as in Bloemfontein . . . that's where it is . . . Bloemfontein . . . on Naval Hill.'

For a moment it appears as if he has lost his train of thought. Marius scratches a match across the side of the box and lights another cigarette. 'In Bloemfontein . . . next weekend . . . a group will get together on Naval Hill. Friday night. And . . . three of you guys . . . can also go. That's what I have organised for you guys.' He waits for his words to sink in.

'Geez, Marius,' a voice says in admiration from somewhere in the circle. 'You're a great pal.'

Marius lifts his hand theatrically. 'I will appoint the three. Tonight. The three that can go.' The teenagers look at each other in excitement, unaware of the dried blood on their arms. 'I've organised a lift and all,' Marius says. Then he gets up to change the music on the turntable. This time it's Duran Duran's 'The Union of the Snake'.

Marius moves about the group as the evening progresses. They don't talk much because words are superfluous on this night of truth, where music, blood and dagga unite them. It's nearly midnight when Marius goes and stands behind Liz-marie and puts his hand on her shoulder. She turns her head. He winks at her and nods his head. She smiles. She's in. Later he does the same with Brenda. And then with Engela. She feels the excitement tingling through her body. Next Friday night . . . they will be on Naval Hill.

Eleven

'Here I am! Over here!' Engela shouts at the group of people crowding below the tree. They push to the front to get a better view of the notice that's nailed to the trunk. It says 'LOST' in big fat letters. Groups of unfamiliar people are gathering around the trees to read the notices. She stands in front of them and waves her arms, but nobody sees her . . .

*   *   *

'Sammy-Jo! Wake up!'

A strong hand is shaking Engela's shoulder. Somebody saw her, she thinks. 'Sammy-Jo! Wake up!' the voice shouts again. 'It's the middle of the day and you are still asleep!'

'Probably popped too many pills,' another voice says mockingly. The two men laugh. Then one of them claps his hands loudly. 'Come on! I'm not asking you again. Get up!'

Engela wakes slowly and pulls herself up against the bed's headrest. Her eyes flutter anxiously around the room. It's Anthony next to the bed, she realises. Steve is sitting on the dressing table chair. 'There,' Anthony says and shoves a glass of brandy and Coke into her hand. She takes the glass and downs the contents without greeting or thanking him, and then puts it down on the bedside table. The alcohol goes to her head in seconds. 'What's the time?'

'That's what you get from lying in bed all day. You lose track of time.'

'Three o'clock. Sunday afternoon. You'll have to get a good rest tonight because tomorrow night you start working,' Steve says.

'Yes,' Anthony joins in. 'Jacques already has three bookings for you. Very good clients, very good. You are going to coin it, girl, mark my words.'

Engela starts crying. 'But all I want to do is go home. Home!'

'Don't start that shit with me,' Anthony says, annoyed. 'Come on, pull yourself together.'

Engela jumps from the bed in a rage and bangs her fists against Anthony's chest: 'But I don't want to be here! I don't want to! Why can't you understand that?'

The smack across her cheek makes her fall back onto the bed. She wants to get up again but Anthony is on top of her. He pulls her T-shirt over her head. He roughly kneads her breasts as he straddles her. 'There is . . . only one way . . . to control . . . rebellious girls like you,' he pants. 'You have to be broken in . . . when you don't want to listen!'

'Like a disobedient horse,' Steve giggles in the background.

'Show her, Steve, show her what we do to girls who don't want to listen,' Anthony says. He gets off her but holds her down with his left hand. Then Steve moves in. He lifts her buttocks and pulls her panties over her legs and feet with force. She kicks but he is on top of her and pins her legs down on the bed. After Engela's second scream, Anthony's hand covers her mouth. She feels Steve pressing between her legs but his entry is blocked by her dryness. He wets two fingers in his mouth to help him gain entry, and then he pushes his erection hard into her. Anthony's hand suppresses her screams, but not the tears from her eyes. He holds her resisting left hand down with his knee and her right arm with his hand. Steve quickly has his way with her and the two club owners change places so that Anthony can drive his stiffness into her. Engela's body doesn't resist; it just trembles under the assault. She remains motionless on the bed after Anthony's turn.

'Hopefully you are ready now for your first client,' Anthony says as he pulls up his pants. 'You could have made it easier for yourself, you know?'

Steve leaves an unfamiliar pill on the bedside table. 'Take that. It's stronger than the usual ones. And be sure to be ready tomorrow night. Six o'clock.'

Engela keeps her eyes shut. Her face is turned away from the door as the men leave the room. Later she hears them talking in the bar. She swallows the pill with the last bit of brandy from the glass.

*   *   *

Was it later that Sunday night? Or maybe during the night? Maybe it was already Monday morning when she woke up through the haze. She's still naked on the bed but someone has covered her with a blanket, she notices. She listens, but there doesn't seem to be anyone in the club. She leans against the passage wall as she struggles first to get to the bathroom, and then to reach the kitchen. She peeps under the door and sees the sun rising. It has to be Monday morning. She's hungry but feels too nauseous to eat anything. She pours a glass of water and goes back to her room. She takes her diary and pen from her bag and gets back into bed.

Monday, 25 October 1993

I took the pill. It was an amazing feeling, like I was drifting on cotton wool. I could float, I forgot about everything, the hurt and the pain. It was incredible. I was lying there thinking how great it was to feel this way. It's the only thing that makes me feel better in this place because it helps me forget everything and everyone. Nothing and no one could help me in any case. My anger at God is gone and I have pleaded with Him to help me. After they were done they left me on the bed just like that. I closed my eyes and drifted off. My entire body was covered in blue marks, even my scalp hurt and I expected to die. I couldn't think, I couldn't speak, I didn't feel anything, and I was simply waiting to become quiet. And I did. I heard thunder somewhere far off and rain falling on the roof. I died, I closed my eyes yesterday afternoon and I died.

*   *   *

Engela wakes up after a few hours. She feels weird, as if she's gone and somebody else is occupying her body. She is tired of fighting. She looks for more painkillers in the bar and notices it's three o'clock. The girls will be here soon, she has to get ready, she thinks without emotion. She takes a long shower. Her dad and stepmother and the garage parties in Dewetsdorp are just a distant memory. Like something that happened many, many years ago, the details of which she has already forgotten. Survival is the only thing that's going through her head right now. She has to make some money first and then get out

104

of here. Without money she can't do anything. When she closes the shower taps she can hear Jacky and Nadia laughing in the club somewhere. Suddenly she's relieved to hear their voices.

'Hello, you guys!' she calls out in excitement as she enters the room and sees them unpacking.

'Sammy-Jo! Are you okay?' Nadia asks and hugs her.

'Hey, you,' Jacky greets and puts a Bar One in her hand. 'That's for you. We have everything in this club except for sweets.'

'So, tonight you have your first clients, we hear?' Nadia says as she sits down in front of the mirror to brush her hair. 'You must be excited. From now on it's just money money, honey! Look, if you can manage all your clients tonight you'll be fine. Then you'll be used to everything.'

'Remember the two golden rules, Sammy-Jo. Do everything they want you to do and always use a condom.'

Engela nods. She takes one of the outfits they got her last week from the wardrobe. 'Will this one be okay for tonight?' She holds up two matching garments, a tight top and a mini-skirt. Nadia whistles. 'Baby, baby, baby! You are going to look hot in that.'

Jacques peeps into the room a little later, after the older girls have helped Engela with her make-up. 'Hey, Sammy-Jo, how's it going?' he asks, but doesn't wait for a response. 'Are you almost ready? It's seven o'clock.'

'Almost,' Nadia responds. 'Just a few finishing touches here and there, you know. Then it's playtime.'

Jacques laughs at her ingenuity. Then he looks at Engela. 'The bosses want to see you. They are waiting in the office. Can you come straight away?'

Engela nods and follows him down the passage to the wooden door. He knocks three times, turns the knob and motions for Engela to enter. 'Sammy-Jo!' Anthony calls out, all friendly now. He stands in a corner of the office, cigar in one hand, and throws his arms wide as if to embrace her.

'Come, sit down,' the burly George waves generously from the leather couch. Steve, sitting in the chair opposite him, doesn't say anything. Engela's miniskirt rides up over her thigh when she sits down on the chair, crossing her legs.

Anthony stubs his cigar in the ashtray on the coffee table. 'Sammy-Jo, my two partners and I would like to say to you tonight that it is a privilege to have you here at Lady Femmé.' The friendliness drips like honey over his words. 'You have been with us for a week already, but tonight is the first night you'll be working. Congratulations.'

He makes it sound like one hell of an achievement, she thinks.

'And we want you to be very happy at the club,' Steve adds. 'You know it's a privilege for anyone to be working in this club, right? And we only want the best for all of you.'

Engela can't believe her ears. Only yesterday she was raped by these two and now they pretend nothing happened. As if they're the best possible employers ever.

'Look, we know last week was probably . . . how shall I put it . . . a slight adjustment for you,' Anthony continues, unperturbed. 'And yes, there was the odd occasion when you were a little obstinate. But hey, we are cool dudes. Really. So, tell you what: we are prepared to overlook your mistakes. To forgive you, understand? And then we turn over a new leaf tonight.'

Engela has learnt her lesson. She doesn't talk back. Yes, she says when she realises the three partners are expecting a response from her. George takes a sip from his whisky and lights a cigarette. He leans forward to Engela. 'Like Anthony said, Sammy-Jo, the three of us are actually cool dudes. So, we have decided to cut a nice deal with you.' He takes another sip. 'Finish working this week. Be obedient and do everything that's expected of you. Don't talk back. Just do it. Your payment will be generous because you'll be having different clients from Nadia and Jacky. We are going to book you the regulars. And they pay the big money. More than the others. And then you can go home on Friday. With your handbag stuffed with money.'

Engela doesn't say anything; she stares at the pattern on the carpet. The same pattern Pieter was staring at three months ago when Anthony set him an ultimatum for his outstanding debt because he couldn't execute the transaction with Mark, the rich Greek guy from Welkom. And because he couldn't repay the advance. Bring us a girl, Anthony threatened him. Bring us fresh blood, otherwise you'll drown in your own blood. If he could do this for them they would forget about the ugly mess. It was the one agreement Pieter had kept. By chance, really, because Engela walked into the workshop at Nick's Auto Repairs in Oranjesig with her brother two months later looking for a job.

'And?' George asks. 'What do you say?'

Engela knows she doesn't have a choice. If it's her only chance to get out of this place, she'll do it. For the sake of survival. 'Yes,' she says. 'It's fine. I'll do it.'

'Clever child. Very clever.' Anthony claps his hands and sits down. 'I'm happy we have an understanding. But let's double check you understand the club rules. Steve, will you?'

'It's actually quite simple, Sammy-Jo. Quite simple,' Steve explains. 'When you work in the evenings you don't leave the bar. You only leave the bar when you go to a room with a client. And remember, don't tell anyone your real name or age, or where you come from. You keep your mouth shut and don't talk about yourself. You do your job and you do what is asked of you. You never, ever go over to the reception area. You stay in the club and do your work.'

'Understood?' Anthony wants to know. 'And Friday you go home.'

Engela nods. There's hope, she thinks. For the sake of her own freedom she can live with this another week. 'Yes,' she says softly. 'It's fine.'

'Good girl. But we can't be sitting around chatting all night, we have to get to work.'

By eight o'clock there are six clients in the bar. Nadia and Jacky flirt with them while Engela sits alone at the end of the counter. George pours her a glass of red wine. A week, and then it will all be over. She hears the doorbell ringing again a little later and Jacques opening the security gate and greeting someone. A man in a dark suit, cream shirt and matching tie appears in the bar area after a few moments. Anthony quickly walks over to the man and shakes his hand heartily. He motions with his head in Engela's direction. The men exchange a few words before Anthony leads him around the counter and introduces him to Engela. She smiles sweetly when he takes her hand but she doesn't pay attention to his name. For some or other reason she has no need to know who he is; all she knows is that the man sitting on the bar-stool next to her is going to be her first client. She asks him what he would like to drink, the way Nadia and Jacky taught her the week before, and places the order with George. She looks him over; at least he looks decent, she thinks. He talks softly in a deep voice and tells her she's prettier than he had imagined. His hand strokes her bare leg while Engela makes eye contact with Nadia on the opposite side of the bar. Nadia winks and gives her the thumbs up. Everything will be fine, the gesture is supposed to indicate. The man explains that he isn't a regular but that Anthony had called him the week before with the news that there's a new girl at the club and he should pop in tonight. He is privileged to be her first client. Engela drinks her red wine faster than usual and immediately orders another round for the two of them, even though his glass is still quite full. But now that he has seen her he will have to pop in more frequently, he continues.

She nods when he takes his packet of cigarettes from his jacket pocket and asks her if she smokes. He lights two cigarettes and hands her one. Across the bar Nadia mingles with two clients. She throws her head back voluptuously when she laughs and gives both of them a kiss on the cheek. It looks like she's enjoying herself, Engela thinks. He will make it worth her while, the man says as they sit smoking. If, and this is a big if, she makes it worth his while, he emphasises. On the one hand she'd like for them to go to one of the little rooms and get it over and done with, but on the other hand she's scared and wants to put it off as long as she can. She motions to George to refill her glass. The security gate opens and closes and two more clients enter and take their seats at the bar. Nadia goes up to them, says hello and asks them what they'd like to drink. Jacky appears from the back rooms with the guy she's been busy with for the last hour hot on her heels. Let's go, Engela suddenly says to the man in the dark suit sitting next to her stroking her leg. She takes a quick sip of her wine and gets up. The man follows her into the second room, where Engela closes the door behind them. She lies down on the single bed and watches the man take his jacket off and hang it on the coat hanger against the wall. Then he loosens his tie and hangs it neatly over his jacket. He unbuttons his shirt slowly while staring at Engela.

'You are beautiful, Sammy-Jo,' he says. 'Truly something special to look at.' He removes his shirt and hangs it on the second coat hanger. His trousers and underpants follow. His lust is at half-mast.

Engela starts crying. Completely unexpectedly. Neither she nor the naked man standing in front of her were expecting this. The tears just come, as do her words: 'Sir, I don't belong here. They are locking me up inside of here. Please, sir, call the police,' she pleads through the tears.

'What? What are you saying?' He doesn't move, though his lust loses even more of its perkiness.

'It's true, sir . . . they are keeping me locked up . . . I don't want to be here!'

The man who would have been her first client turns to his clothes hanging against the wall. Underpants, trousers and then his shirt. His fingers tremble doing up his shirt buttons.

'I have to get out of here . . . sir, I am just a child, sir! Just call the police so they will come and get me!'

'I don't believe this.' He shakes his head. 'I bloody well don't believe what I'm hearing! Do you know . . . do you know . . .' Then he's out the door.

'Help me, sir! Please help me!' Engela calls after him as he disappears quickly down the passage.

'Where's Anthony?' he asks George at the bar.

'In the office. Why?'

'Go call him.'

Engela sits on the single bed in the room, crying into her hands. She wonders what to do next. Should she go back to the bar and wait casually for the police to arrive? But what will she tell her bosses when they want to know where her client disappeared to so fast? Maybe she should just stay in the room. If someone comes asking, she'll say she doesn't know where he went; he said he was going to the bathroom and she had to wait for him. Yes, that's all she'll do, she thinks. She bolts the door. The minutes go by. She wonders how long it will take the police to come and save her. Maybe an hour, maybe a little longer. She regrets not bringing her glass of red wine to the room. She gets a fright when someone bumps against the door from the outside. A couple of hard knocks follow and again somebody bumps against the door, trying to open it. Wow, could they be that quick? Engela gets up and goes to the door. She stands with her hand on the bolt for a few moments before opening it. The door bursts open. Anthony stands in front of her, heaving with anger. Behind him she sees her first client casually leaning against the wall with his arms folded. But what is he doing here? Isn't he supposed to call the police? Then she sees the grin on his face.

Engela doesn't see the first blow coming. She only feels her cheek burning as she falls backwards onto the bed. Anthony pulls her up for the second blow. And then the third. She drops in a heap on the ground. This is where Jacky, Nadia and Jacques discover her five minutes later, after Anthony orders them to fix her up, as she will be working that night. Jacques carries her over his shoulder to the bathroom and props her up in front of the basin.

'Shit, Sammy-Jo? Are you all right, girl?' Jacques inquires. Her trembling body clings to his arm.

Nadia wipes the blood running from her nose with a cloth. 'You have screwed up tonight, Sammy-Jo,' she says sternly. 'Big time.'

'There, drink that,' Jacky says and hands her a pill and a glass of water. Engela swallows. Her legs teeter but Jacques holds her up. When her face is clean he picks her up again and carries her to the room. He puts her down on the bed and Jacky immediately undresses her. Nadia gets a fresh set of clothes from the wardrobe and sits behind Engela to brush her hair.

'I . . . I thought he . . . he would help me,' she tries to explain through the sobbing. 'To get out of here.'

'Oh, don't be stupid, Sammy-Jo!' It's the first time the girls have argued with Engela. They are angry with her because they are losing a precious hour that could have generated income.

'I thought he would . . . call the police.'

Nadia looks at Jacques standing in the door. 'Oh for heaven's sake! Tell her, Jacques,' she motions with her head.

'You have made life very difficult for yourself, Sammy-Jo, very difficult,' he says so softly that Engela can barely hear him. He looks down the passage to check that they are still alone.

'Tell her, Jacques, tell her who her client was.'

'You see, Sammy-Jo, this guy is friends with the boss. Big pals. They scratch each other's backs. He is high up somewhere. We don't know where for sure, but it must be high up. He's the one who sees to it that the police never come bother us at the club, and then you go and ask him to call the police, of all things!' Jacques bursts out laughing. 'You know, if this entire situation wasn't so sad, it would be quite funny. I mean, asking him of all people to call the police!'

'Stop it, Jacques. We're wasting time. And money.' Jacky is irritated. She applies an extra layer of lipstick to Engela's lips to cover up the cut. The bruise above her left breast she covers with base.

'Anyway, in return Anthony assists with other stuff. I don't know exactly what, but once a month he comes around and then he and the boss meet in the office for a long time. And he only wears the latest and most expensive clothes.'

'If you ask me, I think the boss is helping him out with drugs,' Nadia declares.

112

'Hmm, could be,' Jacques agrees. 'Quite possibly.'

'Come, sister, get up so you can get dressed,' Jacky commands. And then to Jacques: 'Be a darling and go get Sammy-Jo a double brandy quickly. Just to bring on the pill, please man.'

Engela stands up. She can hear the others talking as from a distance – as if their bodies are right in front of her, but their voices come floating from a far-off place. She doesn't care; it doesn't matter what happens to her. She lifts her legs to pull on the skirt. Nadia does the zipper at the back and hooks the clip on a clean bra. They dress her in a blouse and fasten the buttons. Somebody hands her a glass of something that she downs quickly. Exactly 48 minutes after Anthony's fists struck her the girls are ready. Nadia and Jacky link arms with Engela and walk down the passage to the front. There's big applause coming from the seven men now sitting in the bar when the three girls appear, but Engela is only vaguely aware of this.

'Party time, guys!' Nadia laughs enticingly.

'Bring it on, bring it on!' someone shouts . . .

* * *

The next afternoon, while Nadia and Jacky are still sitting in front of the television watching *The Silence of the Lambs*, Engela gets out of bed. Slowly she leafs through her diary to a clean page after her last entry. She starts writing:

Tuesday, 26 October 1993
After my last client left last night I looked at the clock. It had just gone half past one. Tired, hurt and broken I dropped onto the bed. Jacky and Nadia also got in, the three of us shared the double bed. None of us said any-

thing, the music stopped playing and then everything was quiet. I closed my eyes and fell asleep. This morning Jacky woke me up with a glass and headache pills, as well as the white pill. I drank the pills. I felt raw, my head aching and every muscle in my body hurt. Next to me was a wad of money. I started counting it. On my first night and the promise of getting out of there, I made R500. I put the money in my suitcase. The girls had something to celebrate, they reached their target for the night, made enough money, but the rest of the week was still ahead. They were saying how happy they were it had been a good night. I got up and took a shower. Jacky made us breakfast. Later I joined them in the television room where they were busy watching something. Jacky put her arms around me and asked if I was okay, I just shook my head as the tears came running down. The girls were probably told to keep a watch on me all the time and that I wasn't allowed to go out, because they tried everything to keep me happy, but never did they ask me who I was and where I came from. We spent the entire morning and afternoon in front of the television. Jacky and Nadia are watching the last movie now before we have to get ready. I am looking forward to the end of the week when I will be free.

Twelve

That Friday afternoon the routine starts as usual. They shower, do their make-up and Nadia does Engela's hair. Engela has sensed how the other two are becoming more motherly towards her; they have tried all week to make her laugh and relax. She wonders if they know that tonight will be her last night. At seven o'clock – an hour before the doors open – George brings them double whiskies on ice. Just a little appetiser, he jokes. Engela downs her drink the way she has done every night over the last week.

'No, sister, slow down,' Nadia scolds her playfully.

Engela giggles. 'I have to, man, I have to. It's the only way I'll survive tonight.'

Nadia knows, because later in the evening she smuggles half a bottle of whisky into Engela's room. There are three men in the room doing their thing and leaving their mark between Engela's legs; in between she pours one drink after the other. Only until tonight, she repeats over and over in her mind. Only tonight . . . tomorrow I go home . . . home . . . then I'll be free.

This Friday is quieter than usual: Engela has had three

clients, but Jacky and Nadia only one each. It isn't even eleven and yet the club is empty. Disappointed and tipsy, Nadia and Jacky sit themselves down at the bar counter for a nightcap before Engela joins them. She wonders if she should say good-bye to them. She won't be seeing them ever again. But one thing she's learnt systematically over the past two weeks is to speak as little as possible. And George behind the bar is already looking at her suspiciously. She's still wondering why when he pours her a drink as well.

'You Joburg girls have to get ready, the taxi will be here soon,' Jacques calls from the reception hall.

'Shit, yes!' Nadia says and nips her half-smoked cigarette in the ashtray before going to the toilet and then the room to collect her and Jacky's baggage. They have to be at the bus terminal behind the Free State Stadium before half past twelve to catch the Greyhound back to Johannesburg. Engela takes the half-smoked cigarette from the ashtray and lights it. Outside she can hear the taxi hooting and Jacques opening the security gate. George is sitting opposite her on a bar-stool, but he's completely plastered.

'Bye, you!' the girls shout in unison as they walk briskly through the bar towards the front door. For a moment Engela considers rushing out the door with them. She'll be gone before Jacques can stop her, and in any case George is too drunk to react. But is she herself sober enough to rush into the dark night? No, she's not. She also can't leave behind her suitcase with all her stuff and the money she's been handed every morning. It's only a few more hours; when the sun rises she'll be free. Jacques locks the front door and the gate and says goodnight. He disappears into the kitchen to go out by the back door to the parking area.

George is also getting ready to leave and is looking for his car keys, which he left on the bar shelves behind him earlier that evening.

'Can I have another one?' Engela asks, huskily, and pushes her empty glass across the bar counter.

'Help yourself,' George mumbles. 'I'm pissing off.' He exits by the back door, which is also locked with double padlocks.

Engela's eyes travel over the bottles on the shelves. As it is her last night she might as well spoil herself a little bit, she thinks. The spoiling comes in the shape of a bottle of Southern Comfort and a can of Sprite that she takes with her to the bedroom. The next morning the booze is unopened beside the bed when she wakes up, still dressed. She hears someone in the bar, who then goes to the kitchen and turns on a tap. She notices the wad of money on the dressing table, like every morning the past week. One of the three bosses must be here already, she realises. It's Saturday, she sighs thankfully. Saturday at last! The day of her release. She grabs the money on the dressing table, along with the bundle in her suitcase, and stacks it next to her. Within minutes she stares in disbelief at the pile of R100 notes – R2 500 in one week! They weren't lying when they said she was going to make a lot of money, she thinks, as she puts the money back in her suitcase. She goes to the bathroom to take a shower and wash away the finger-marks on her body from the night before. She has to be clean when she goes out this afternoon to rent herself a flat. It's what Mr de Wet had taught her six years ago at the plot outside Bloemfontein: a girl always has to smell nice, she remembers him saying, as the hot water runs down her body. She wants a flat above the Westdene Café and Takeaways in Barnes Street and to be able to go downstairs every morning with a new R20 note to buy a small bottle of milk for R1.50 from the rude Greek owner. Until he gets fed up with her because he's run out of change, Engela giggles in the shower. That'll teach him. Chasing her away because she couldn't work with money.

After showering, she puts on a pair of jeans, a T-shirt and a light jacket. Her mum bought her the jacket at the beginning of the year, two weeks before she died. It's quiet inside the club; the boss who was here just now has probably gone somewhere quickly before he will come back and let her go, she thinks. She sits in front of the mirror and blow-dries her hair the way Nadia has taught her. Then the make-up, just a whole lot less than what Jacky has applied the past two weeks. Half an hour later there's still no one in the club. Engela hopes they're not running late because she has very important things to do this afternoon. First the flat, and then tomorrow she'll go to Checkers at the Sanlam Mall to get a few essentials. A pot and a pan, knives and forks, and some popcorn. Oh, and cooking oil. She craves popcorn. And a milkshake. On Monday she'll give Pieter at Nick's Auto a call to come and give her a hand with furniture and curtains; he promised to help her when she has a lot of money. And now she has all of R2 500. Later, she waits on the couch in the bar, her packed suitcase next to her. The minutes on the clock slowly tick away. It's half past eleven. Hell, where can Anthony be? Or Steve, or George? Engela battles the urge for a drink; she knows she can't go renting a flat this afternoon when she's tipsy. Maybe just a small one? After twenty minutes she gives in and pours herself a brandy and Coke. Just a single with her daily pain pill in the morning. Then another single.

After an hour or so she hears the key turn in the kitchen door, and then the padlock on the gate. Engela gets up and grabs her suitcase; they can leave straight away, she thinks. There is no reason to wait. She won't ask Anthony to drop her in Westdene; she just wants to get out of here. She's not afraid of walking, in any case. But it's Steve, with two Chinese girls on his heels.

'Sammy-Jo! Afternoon!' he greets her. 'How's it going?' He turns to the girls behind him: 'This is Chan and Bao. Please go show them the bathroom and the single rooms, and then come to the front.'

Engela is stunned for a moment, but then she realises the girls are her replacements. Steve shoves the girls in Engela's direction. 'Go. Go with Sammy-Jo.'

They are slightly older than her, Engela guesses. Maybe twenty or twenty-one. 'Come,' she beckons to them. They look at each other in bewilderment before following Engela. She's not quite sure who's Chan and who's Bao, and she soon discovers they don't speak much English. She shows them the bathroom and the little rooms, where they each get onto a single bed, without saying a word, and sit right up against the back wall, startled. Steve is waiting for Engela in the bar.

'We can go,' she says and lifts her suitcase again.

Steve doesn't move. 'Sorry?'

'I'm ready. We can go.'

'And where do you want to go, if I may ask?'

'Out. Away. To the city,' Engela responds.

'And what about work?'

'But . . . it's Saturday . . . the week has gone and you guys said another week and I can go. So . . . that's what I mean. I'm ready to go, you can unlock.'

Steve takes out a cigar. He takes his time as he turns it around and looks at it from all sides before pressing it between his lips and striking a match. 'But didn't Anthony tell you last night that you will have to stay a little longer?'

Engela lowers her suitcase to the floor. 'What?' Her voice is shaking. 'How? . . . I mean, no.'

The sweet smell of cigar smoke hangs heavily in the bar. Steve clicks his tongue. 'Oh dear, oh dear,' he says, almost pityingly. 'That he would forget about something so important. But then again, he was also quite busy last night in his office. He has many deals to keep track of, you know.'

'Why? You said that . . .' It suddenly dawns on Engela that she won't be leaving here today. Disheartened, she can feel the tears behind her eyes. 'Only a week . . . that's what you said! Only a week! And I kept my side of the agreement.'

'Calm down, Sammy-Jo, calm down. It won't help much shouting at me. The plans have changed slightly, nothing serious. And Anthony forgot to tell you, that's all.'

'How did the plans change? I did what you asked me to do.'

'Business is a funny thing. It changes from day to day, and one has to be prepared for it, do you understand? Especially when you're running a big business like Lady Femmé. Things change around here; you can't be planning too much in advance. Drink?'

Engela shakes her head. 'What . . . what changed?'

'There's a private party tonight. About fifteen guys. The booking only came in on Wednesday, and Nadia and Jack couldn't do it. They have family they see only on weekends, and surely you don't expect them to be staying behind for the weekend just because you want to leave, right?'

'Private party? Tonight . . . and I have to—'

'Not you alone, Sammy-Jo! Not you alone! That's why I brought Chan and Bao to help you. See how good we are to you. Getting you assistants. You should be grateful, you know. And by the way, speaking of which, we haven't heard you once say "thank you" for the money on the dressing table every morning.'

Engela feels an urge to spit at the man sitting in front of

her, but she doesn't. She'll be smacked again, and she's not up for that right now. She turns around, grabs her suitcase and storms to the bedroom. She slams the door behind her before collapsing on the bed, crying. Steve opens the door within seconds.

'The party is starting a little later. They only booked it for nine o'clock. See to it that you and the two Chinese ladies are ready half an hour before the time,' he instructs. 'I have to go now. See you guys tonight.'

Engela only gets up an hour later. She blows her nose. On the way to the toilet she notices the two girls still sitting in the same position. They look scared and hungry. Engela makes them sandwiches of cold meat. When she hands them the plates, they smile and say something in a foreign language. Engela suspects they are thanking her. She wonders where they are from and if they know what will be expected of them tonight. When they were at the kitchen door earlier, waiting for Steve to unlock, did they know what was waiting behind that door? Later, she indicates with hand movements that they should go and shower. She doesn't feel like showering again. She sits in front of the mirror fixing her make-up. Chan and Bao don't have any luggage, not even a handbag. Engela will have to let them use her make-up. She fetches them after they have showered and lets them sit together on the seat in front of the dressing table. They catch on quickly when she points at her make-up kit and then at their faces. While Chan and Bao apply their make-up, Engela gets dressed. The men's party at Lady Femmé starts in just over an hour, but they need to have a couple of strong doubles first.

The group of fifteen men are already intoxicated when they arrive at the club in a boisterous mood, but so are Engela, Chan and Bao. The guys are all pretty young. Younger than the usual clients. In between all the noise and music and hands touching and glasses clinking Engela discovers that tonight is someone's bachelor's party. His stinking-rich dad has given him a blank cheque to celebrate this important day in his life in a fitting manner. Before pulling into the club's parking area in two rented stretch limousines, they had dined at the revolving restaurant next to the Sand du Plessis Theatre. Lip-licking dessert time was what they were looking forward to, which is why they are now throwing back drinks at the Lady Femmé bar while their eager hands feel up the three girls. It doesn't bother them that Chan and Bao can't communicate much; the men haven't come here for intellectual conversation. George and Steve are behind the bar counter pouring the next round of Springbokkies. Jacques and Anthony aren't working tonight.

'Blowjob for Henk! Blowjob for Henk!' chant the partygoers, who will all be in church in three weeks for Henk's wedding ceremony. George immediately mixes a dash of Baileys Irish Cream and Kahlúa in a liqueur glass and squirts whipped cream from a can on top. It's the latest cocktail craze. And of course Henk is not allowed to touch the glass with his hands, the way the craze requires, when George puts it down in front of him on the bar counter. He clamps onto the glass with his teeth, throws his head back and lets the alcohol run down his throat. Everybody claps loudly when he puts the empty glass back down on the bar counter.

'Blowjob for Henk! Blowjob for Henk!' the almost-bridegroom calls out and dramatically drops his trousers to his ankles as his buddies urge him on. Steve pushes Engela forward: 'Go do your job, Sammy-Jo,' he orders and hands her a condom. She kneels in front of Henk, rolling the condom down Henk's stiff manhood the way Jacky taught her. He stands triumphantly with his hands on his hips while his friends cheer on the oral sex display in front of them.

'Suck it, baby, suck it!' Henk moans. And after barely a minute: 'Fuckkkkk!'

Engela removes the condom with her right hand, gets up and throws it away in the bin behind the bar counter. 'Double brandy, George. Now, please,' she asks. He pours and she downs it. The rest of the group are occupying themselves with Chan and Bao, who are also naked by now. They are lying emotionless on the ground with three, four guys all over each of them. Somebody fetches her from behind the bar counter. 'I want to marry you,' he mumbles as one of his hands grips a breast. 'No one gets a girlfriend in this place,' someone else calls out. 'Only a turn!'

It's all over after another hour and a half. Everybody has had their turn. The stag partygoers exit buddy-buddy to the limousines waiting outside. 'That was one helluva night,' one of them says as he hugs Henk. 'Thanks, pal! Check you at the wedding!'

It's quiet inside the club. All that remains is the smell of used condoms, cigarettes and alcohol. And sweat. Steve counts for the third time the wad of banknotes Henk had handed him in an envelope. George starts emptying ashtrays and carrying glasses back to the kitchen. Engela retrieves her clothes from the floor and puts them on. Chan and Bao are sitting on the couch against the wall, their legs pulled up high under their chins, their eyes staring blankly into space. Engela doesn't feel like looking for their clothes as well. She just takes their hands, pulls them up and walks them to a single bed each to sleep in before she gets into her own bed. She can hear the familiar sounds of the back door being locked, and she knows they're alone now; now she can drift off in her dreams. Maybe to that park again, where all those people are looking for her. But tonight she doesn't get to drift off, despite all the alcohol in her body. Later she gets up and pours another drink, just to be sure. She goes through the drawers in the bar and discovers an unknown pill, which she takes. Glass in hand, she walks over to the reception area and listens as always to the noise from outside. She can hear people walking by every now and then. Then she goes back to her room to tear a page from her diary. 'HELP!' she writes, and shoves it under the door towards the pavement. She listens for whether somebody stops and picks it up, somebody who might turn around to figure out where the note came from. She can feel her brain slowly disengaging from her body. God help me, she mutters as she stumbles back to her room. She's barely in bed when a dream takes her back to a hot Friday afternoon in Bloemfontein, in February 1993.

*   *   *

Engela strolls in a daze along with a group of mourners into the Dutch Reformed Church in Fichardt Park. Her father, brother and sister walk in front of her. There are many people inside the church, she notices. Both familiar and unfamiliar faces. Friends and colleagues of her parents, family she hasn't seen in years and a number of school friends from Christiaan de Wet High in Dewetsdorp in their school uniforms. Also people she doesn't know from a bar of soap. Her father indicates they should sit on the left-hand side of the deacons' pews. Joshua, her stepdad, who married her mother in April 1991, is sitting behind them at an angle. Between her and the pulpit is the casket keeping her mother from harm. She's lying there with eyes closed dressed in a beautiful long white dress Engela hasn't seen before. AVBOB's make-up artist has covered up the terrible wound so perfectly that none of the next of kin will be reminded of that Tuesday, 9 February 1993. A bunch of St Joseph lilies decorates the casket. Outside it's raining lightly.

Engela has received many cards these last few days: from the school, the teachers, the neighbours, pupils from school she didn't know, people from town she's only encountered in passing. All the words of sympathy in the cards mean nothing to Engela; all she knows is that she has seen death. Right there on the carpet in her mother's bedroom next to the bed. Otherwise she doesn't understand much. She is a welfare case, nothing more. A welfare case, a welfare case, she whimpers in her dream. Then a policeman enters her dream. He holds a letter out to her. They found it on the scene, he says. It's addressed to her. Engela unfolds the writing paper with her mother's handwriting:

> My dear Engela, I am sorry for doing this. Mummy loves you, but my migraines are driving me crazy. I can't go on like this.
> Mummy loves you very much.
> Xxxxxx
> Mum

*   *   *

It's gone twelve o'clock already when Engela wakes up on Sunday. She is more disoriented than usual and her headache is worse. Her legs shake when she gets up to go to the bar for the painkillers. Then she gets back into bed to continue sleeping – there's nothing to do in any case. What happened last night again? Where are Jacky and Nadia? She's in too much of a daze to remember straight away. What day is it? And Anthony, Steve and George? Or Jacques? She hears voices in her head, faint initially but then the volume increases. Blowjob for Henk! Blowjob for Henk! Then she remembers. It was a private party. Fifteen young men. She looks at the dressing table and notices the money for last night hasn't arrived yet. And then there were these two Chinese girls. Chan and Bao. Where are they? Still asleep? She gets up again and goes to the two single rooms. The first room is empty, the second and the third also. There's no one. Back to the bar. Everything's been cleaned up and packed away after last night's ruckus. Something's not right, but she isn't sure exactly what. Engela sits down cross-legged on the bed before her eye catches her suitcase on the floor. The lid is open. What's going on today? She jumps up and flings her clothes from the suitcase. All her money is gone . . .

Thirteen

Like a wild animal not sure what move to make when the cage door is suddenly flung open. That's how Engela feels when Jacques unlocks the kitchen door and steps aside so she can walk ahead of him. Tentatively, she goes and stands in the parking area. Up above the stars are shining in a cloudless sky.

'It's a beautiful evening, isn't it?' Jacques says behind her when he notices how she stares at the stars. She simply nods. This Thursday evening is the first time in over a month that she can see the sky again. She looks around her, recognising the steel gate through which she and Pieter entered that day in October. Where they parked after he promised her that he had arranged a job for her that would pay a lot of money and where she would be looked after. For the umpteenth time she wonders why he has never come looking for her or at least to check if she is okay. Could it be that he and the club owners are . . .? No, she lets go of the thought immediately. It just cannot be.

After all her money disappeared that Saturday night four weeks ago, she confronted Anthony. He just shrugged his shoulders. It will teach her not to keep so much money in her suitcase, he said. But there's another problem, he added. Because she has no money saved, they can't let her go just like that. Surely not. She'll have no money, food or a place to stay, and he could never live with that. He's a nice dude and he cares about her, right? Luckily he has a solution: she can continue working at the club a little while longer. A few more months until she has enough money saved up to go far away and enjoy her life, he said. She stormed out of his office in a rage and refused to get ready for work that Monday night. Nadia and Jacky pleaded with her: please, do as they say, otherwise you'll be smacked again. After a while she reluctantly agreed, but she had learnt her lesson. Never again would she leave money in her suitcase. Systematically she went about creating hiding places in her room: first she put the folded banknotes under the wooden trim in front of the curtain rail, and then in the spaces between the shelves in the wardrobe. She also cut a hole in the mattress and bundled some of the money in there. And this evening, Thursday, 25 November, she's standing outside the club in the parking area for the first time. Somebody staying at a hotel has booked her; over the last few weeks she has proved herself so devoted to the club that she's allowed to take the booking. Anthony has even praised her.

'Yes, that's right,' Engela reacts to Jacques's comment. 'I haven't seen the stars in a long while. I have forgotten what they look like. But maybe . . . maybe this is the first time in my life that I really notice and appreciate them.'

Jacques opens the passenger door for her to get in. Maybe tonight's my chance to jump out and run away, Engela thinks while Jacques walks round the car and gets in behind the steering wheel. He turns to her as if reading her mind: 'Sammy-Jo, listen to me carefully. Don't do anything silly or irresponsible. Don't try and jump out while I'm driving; you will only get hurt really badly, that's all. And don't try and run away either. The bosses will get you, believe me. They have many contacts here. Also . . . they don't have a problem with making a person disappear.'

He starts the engine and proceeds to the heavy steel gate. Before pressing the remote he turns to her. 'I don't want worse things happening to you than what's already going on, Sammy-Jo. Please?'

He's always been good and decent to her, but for the first time she can hear the concern in his voice. He presses the remote and the gate opens. He turns left, drives round the block and heads in a westerly direction. 'The guys booking girls from their hotel rooms are usually nice,' Jacques says a little later. 'They don't take chances, so there's nothing to worry about. You'll be fine.'

As they approach Brandwag, he says: 'Anyway, I'll be waiting in the bar downstairs. If you're not back in an hour, I'll come see if you're okay.'

He turns right into the parking lot of the Southern Sun hotel. After turning off the engine he turns to her again: 'Please, Sammy-Jo, don't try anything funny,' he says, his voice serious. 'Both of us will be in big trouble with the bosses. You have no idea.'

She nods. She's wearing a formal black dress Anthony got her this morning, along with her matching high heels and a shiny necklace that glitters around her neck. 'Don't be silly!' Nadia laughed earlier on when Engela wanted to know if they were real diamonds. If she wasn't a prostitute she would almost feel like a lady right now, Engela thought as she put the dress on. It seems Jacques is quite familiar with the hotel because he walks past the reception desk on the left in the direction of one of the corridors leading from the lobby. He greets one of the hotel staff walking past them with a nod. Engela's heels sink into the thick, soft carpeting. It's a long passage with no end to it. They pass a gym where three people are busy cycling. Then they go up a flight of stairs. The passage curves to the right before Jacques knocks on the door of room 228. He steps aside immediately so that Engela is standing at the door by herself. The door opens. A tall man, probably in his thirties she thinks, stands in front of her. She puts her hand out. 'Good evening, sir. I'm Sammy-Jo,'

He takes her hand and says: 'Louis. Pleased to meet you. Please, come inside.'

Engela has never seen such a fancy room before. As she steps into it she glimpses a white-tiled bathroom to the right. In the main area there's a queen-sized bed flanked by two bedside tables. The small bedside lights create an almost romantic atmosphere. She'll soon be on her back on that bed, she realises suddenly. There are two armchairs either side of a coffee table close to some sliding doors that open onto a brightly lit swimming pool. One day, when she's left the club, she will also live in such a smart place, Engela thinks.

'Sit down,' Louis says and points at one of the chairs. 'Bubbly?'

He doesn't wait for her answer and immediately takes the bottle of JC le Roux from the ice bucket on the table and pours a glass for each of them. Nice to meet you, he repeats as he passes her the glass. Engela folds her legs elegantly under the evening dress the way Jacky has shown her. Remember, Jacky always says, even if you are a prostitute you are still a lady.

'You seem really young,' Louis says as he sits down. 'How old are you?'

'Twenty-one,' Engela lies immediately. 'I just look very young.'

'Then we drink to our eternal youth,' he says with a smile

and lifts his glass. Engela does the same and laughs politely. Then it becomes quiet between them. 'I like Bloemfontein,' he says, unexpectedly. 'But I'm from Cape Town, actually. It's where I grew up. I attended Paarl Gimnasium. Stayed in Mc-Farlane hostel. My parents live in Camps Bay and I work for my dad's business. It's a brokerage. He has offices in Cape Town and Stellenbosch. And the two of us opened another branch here in Bloemfontein two months ago. That's why I'm here. Business.'

Engela is not quite sure what to do next. This is unfamiliar territory to her: in the club you get booked, you go to the room, get undressed, open your legs, the guy does his thing and you're done. But now she's sitting in an evening dress and drinking bubbly in a luxurious hotel room with someone telling her about his schooldays and his work.

'Should I . . . get undressed?' she asks half-heartedly after twenty minutes, pointing at her clothes.

'No! Please, no!' Louis says. He gets up to fill their glasses. 'I'm just looking for company. Don't feel like being alone tonight.'

'But actually I never wanted to work with policies and that kind of stuff,' he continues when he sits down again. 'I wanted to become a doctor, but my father said no, I have to become involved with the business so that I can take it over from him one day when he retires.'

He leans over to her. 'I actually hate my job. But I never had a choice. You know, I didn't even want to attend Gimmies. But I had to. My dad said it would be good for me.' He twirls the glass in his hands and takes small sips. Engela's glass is empty long before his every time, but then he refills hers. One for him, three for her.

'And you?' he asks. 'Why do you do this type of work?'

Engela's heart starts beating. Maybe she can trust this man.

Maybe she should tell him everything and ask him for his help. He could sneak her out a back door without Jacques noticing. Or he could hide her in this room and tell Jacques she ran away. She could hide under the bed. But she doesn't say anything. All the threats she got from her bosses, the warnings from Nadia, Jacky and Jacques, make her keep quiet. 'Just like you . . . I also have to,' she responds. 'Do the work. It's our jobs.'

Now, Engela, now, it rages inside her. This is your chance to get away. Then the fear: what if they find her; what will they do to her then? Life doesn't always turn out the way you thought it would when you were a child, she hears Louis say.

After an hour there's a knock on the door. Louis glances at his watch. 'I guess my time is up,' he says and gets up. She gets up too. 'Will it be okay if you stay another hour?' he asks.

Yes, please, she exults on the inside. She doesn't feel like going back to the club right now. 'It's fine, sir . . . Louis,' she tells the broker from Cape Town.

*   *   *

'Let's stop for a milkshake, please, Jacques?' Engela asks on their way back to the club two hours later. 'There's a roadhouse around here somewhere.'

Jacques looks at her. 'What?'

'Oh please, man, I want a milkshake so badly. Chocolate. Double thick. I've only been drinking alcohol these past few weeks.'

He shakes his head. 'Do you want to go and take chances?'

'No! I behaved myself. You can trust me,' she responds. 'It's just . . . it's just . . . that I suddenly have this hectic craving for a milkshake.'

Jacques laughs. 'Milkshake! Of all things! You're not trying to get me into trouble, are you?'

She shakes her head. 'No! I promise! Come on, man, please?'

'Okay then. But remember—'

'Yes, I know. I know the rules. I won't do anything funny.'

Jacques laughs again and turns into Zastron Street one block up. Moments later he pulls into the roadhouse parking area.

'We'll tell Anthony the battery ran flat. I left the headlights on or something,' Jacques says after ordering two milkshakes. 'And we had to ask people to help push the car. He will want to know why we are fifteen minutes late. You'll have to help cover, Sammy-Jo.'

Engela nods her head. 'Of course I will. How else?'

They observe in silence the waiters running between the cars with their white wire trays. It's already eleven in the evening but there are still quite a number of cars around. Mostly students coming for a late-night snack or a break from hostel food. Neil Diamond's 'Beautiful Noise' is coming from metal speakers attached to the outside walls.

'I like the oldies,' Jacques says.

Engela smiles. 'My brother used to play that single over and over in his bedroom.'

Surprised, Jacques turns to her. 'You have a brother?'

She nods.

'Who . . . where does he stay? Does he know . . . where you are?'

She shakes her head. 'No, I don't think he knows. Or maybe he does. I don't know. I really don't know what to think. I am . . . just confused, Jacques. Everything is just really messed up.'

'But your brother. Where is he? And . . . your parents. Where are they?'

She can hear the concern in his voice, but she's still too

scared. She waits for the waiter to bring their milkshakes in two cardboard cups before she answers him. 'Why do you ask? You know I'm not allowed to answer that. Or talk to anybody about it. Otherwise I get smacked again. Do you want to get me into trouble now?'

Jacques sighs. 'Look, I trusted you tonight. I said fine, let's stop at the roadhouse. Surely that shows you can trust me as well? I actually know nothing about you.'

Engela uses a plastic spoon for her milkshake because the double thick is just too thick to suck through the straw. 'And I actually know nothing about you,' she responds.

'Ha-ha, yes okay, you got me there. You're right. So basically the two of us know nothing about each other. Then we're equal. So, who goes first? You or me?'

Engela is assured of what she has suspected for a while now: she can trust Jacques. But she remains careful. A vicious hiding will make anyone apprehensive. 'You first,' she says.

'Thought you might say that,' he says while glancing at the clock on the dashboard. Another fifteen minutes and they're out of there, otherwise both of them will be in trouble with their bosses tonight.

'Mine is a long story, Sammy-Jo . . .'

'Not as long as mine.'

'Maybe, maybe not?' Their milkshakes are still half full when he starts the car and steers towards the street.

'I'll tell you what. Next Saturday morning I have to come in early to do the books. One of the bosses unlocks the doors for me around nine, but then disappears until I phone to say I'm done. Let's chat then. But then you mustn't start boozing again for breakfast.'

'Deal!' Engela giggles. 'Deal.' She swallows the last of the milkshake when they stop in front of the sliding gate at the club.

'One more question. How old are you really?' Jacques plays with the remote in his hand.

This time Engela doesn't think, she just answers him: 'Sixteen.'

Jacques stops playing with the remote. 'Good heavens, Sammy-Jo! Really?'

'Yes.'

'I thought you lied to me . . . that day when you turned up at the club for the first time. You said you were twenty-one. But sixteen?' He slaps the steering wheel. 'Shit, man.'

He presses the green button. The gate opens slowly and then closes behind them.

Fourteen

Beep, beep, beep, the calculator sounds as Jacques enters the numbers. He doesn't really understand why he has to complete a statement of income and expenses every month. It's not as if the club owners are loyal taxpayers who will show the statements to the Receiver with pride. But Anthony insists. He always says, if you don't know the state of your business you might as well close your doors, because then you don't have a business. That's why Jacques is sitting at his desk in the reception area, as he does the first Saturday of every month, entering figures in the A4 book with the black cover.

He writes 'November 1993' at the top of the page and draws four columns from top to bottom. Then he pages through the journal next to him containing client information from every evening. Next to each name he enters the amount they spent in the bar, as well as which girl they booked and how much they paid for her, and then the girl's commission for the night. His fingers track the entries with Sammy-Jo's name first. Eighty clients, he notices, is what she had last month. It doesn't include the bachelor party, because the bosses didn't keep track that particular evening. Beep-beep, times 80, times 125 commission per client. Beep-beep-beep, goes the calculator as the total increases and grows to R10 000. That's how much money she made last month. Jacques wonders what she's doing with all the money, because she can't go out and spend it. He also doesn't know about the R2 500 that was stolen after her first week.

'Don't forget our appointment tomorrow morning, okay?' he quickly whispered to Engela last night after checking that the bosses' attention was elsewhere. She just smiled, took a sip from her brandy and lit a cigarette. It was a few minutes after eleven and her last client for the evening had just left.

'And don't sit around drinking until some ungodly hour, otherwise you won't be up early in the morning.' He looked around to see if George was busy in the kitchen before he said, half-jokingly: 'I want you in reception at ten, on the dot, okay?'

'Yes, go on, you,' she laughed. 'Get lost so I can go to bed.'

But this morning he heard her bedroom door open only after ten. When Steve unlocked for him earlier, Jacques had said he would be a little longer than usual because there were some figures in the journal that didn't add up. His ears follow her footsteps to the bathroom, then back to the bedroom and later to the kitchen, where she lingers between the tap, the kettle and the refrigerator door for a while. When she enters the reception area with two mugs of coffee Jacques' fingers are still punching away at the calculator.

'Morning,' she says, sleepily. 'I made coffee.'

'Morning? It's nearly afternoon, young lady, but thanks for the coffee.'

'Please, Jacques, I have a headache. Don't give me a hard time.' She sits cross-legged on the two-seater couch across from Jacques' desk. She's wearing a long white T-shirt, with a teddy-bear print, over sleeping shorts. She gulps down the coffee, holding the mug with both hands.

'That guy in the hotel . . . you know, he didn't treat me like a prostitute even once,' she says out of the blue. 'We didn't even do it. He just wanted to talk. That's what he paid for. Just to have somebody to talk to. Nothing more. Nothing! Just talk. That . . . that gave me a bit of hope again, if I can put it that way?'

'Yes, Sammy-Jo . . . I don't know . . . but hell, when you told me you are sixteen . . . shit, that got to me. That's bad. What are you doing here? What's your story?'

'Our deal was, you first,' she answers in between gulps of coffee.

'Yes, but what are you doing here?'

Engela explodes all of a sudden: 'Do you think I'm here because I want to be?' she yells at him. 'Do you think I came to this fucking place to be locked up and get screwed and beaten up? Is that what you think? Tell me, is that what you think?'

'Sammy-Jo, Sammy-Jo, please, I didn't mean it that way. All I mean is—'

'Mean's arse. What are you doing here? You don't get locked up. Why are you here? You don't have to come back?'

'I don't have much of a choice. Really, I don't. I have to do it . . . I have to!'

'God damn it!' Engela shouts and jumps up. 'Have to! Have to! You don't know what you're talking about!' In the kitchen she discards the rest of her coffee, grabs two painkillers from the bar and goes back to her bedroom in a rage. In the background she can hear Jacques adding up last month's profits. Her body is shaking with disgust. Who the hell does he think he is, telling her he has no other choice but to work in this place? Grmph! Her erratic breathing and pulsating headache subside after about ten minutes, but her body is still shaking. She gets up and walks back to the bar. 'Sammy-Jo?' She hears Jacques calling her, but she ignores him. She pours a double Klipdrift in a tall glass, fills it with ice and grabs a Coke from the refrigerator. That's what she needs right now. She slams the bedroom door so hard that the sound reverberates through the empty club.

Half an hour later, Jacques knocks on her bedroom door. 'Sammy-Jo? Can I come in?' She doesn't answer him, but he opens the door and sits down on the seat in front of the dressing table. 'Sammy-Jo, I don't know—'

She holds out her empty glass to him, calmer now. 'Another one. Please?'

The signs of her rage are visible in her reddened eyes. 'It's early still. Not even one o'clock,' he says. 'Don't you want something to eat rather? Can I go buy you a hamburger?'

She doesn't lower her glass. 'Please? Brandy. Make it a double.'

He takes the glass and goes to the bar. Geez, why is life so screwed up? Why did he ever allow himself to end up in this place? The money? The same reason everyone else ends up working here. The money. He's not a regular boozer, but he pours himself a brandy and Coke as well. Even if it's not even one o'clock. In three months, at the end of February, he'll be gone. Last month he wrote the final papers of his BAcc degree at Kovsies and has already secured an internship at Malan Accountants in the city. Soon he won't be needing this place's money; then he's out of here, he thinks, as he adds ice to their drinks. But what about Sammy-Jo?

'Sorry,' Engela says later in the bedroom, after taking four sips from her drink. Four sips for the four different places she has hidden the bundles of R50 and R20 notes. 'I don't know why I was so silly. It's . . . just . . . this place.'

'It's okay.'

'You asked me, so now I can ask you. How old are you, Jacques? But don't lie.'

'You lied, the first time.'

'Had to.'

'Yes, sure, maybe you had to.' He takes another sip from his drink and then another without looking at her. Only then does he say 'Twenty-three'.

She laughs. 'Also a spring chicken. And you lecture me!'

Their conversation consists of short sentences broken by extended pauses. Slowly, they rebuild the mutual trust shattered earlier. But after the third round Jacques starts talking. Typically for someone with a brain for mathematics, he summarises his life story in a few sentences.

A child from a farm in the Brandfort district. That's where he grew up. An only child. Then that Christmas day in 1983 when he was thirteen years old. They had attended church in town, after which his father started a fire for a braai in the small lapa next to the farmhouse and his mother prepared things to eat in the kitchen. That was when the farm attackers came. His dad died in the lapa. Jacques was in the Universitas Hospital for three weeks, his mother for two months. Initially she rented out the farm, but had to sell it eventually to cover all the medical expenses. After six months of physical therapy the injury to his left leg healed, but his mother's crushed hipbone confined her to a wheelchair. Four years later, just after his seventeenth birthday, she died in her sleep. People said she died mourning her husband. The government placed him in the Memorial Children's Home in Ladybrand because there were no family members who could take care of him.

'Next round?' Jacques asks when he finishes his story. Both their glasses are empty.

'Yes, but you're not really done, you know.'

'Then you'll have to ask what you still want to know,' he replies before walking to the bar.

'How did you end up here? I mean, in this club?' she asks after five minutes.

'I always wanted to go study. BAcc. Mathematics and numbers fascinate me. The way adding up a few figures can create a picture of a business. Geez, it's nice.'

Engela laughs. 'You know, two months ago I worked in a café for a couple of days. The Greek dude fired me because he said I couldn't add and subtract.'

Jacques grins. 'Cheers,' he says and lifts his glass. 'To the stupid Greek dude.'

'But you haven't told me why you work here.'

He plays with the ice cubes in his glass. 'Yes, I often wonder about that one. Sometimes you think you don't have a choice, but maybe there's another option you just don't notice. Or sometimes the choice you make is just not the right one.'

'No, Jacques, you're talking in circles. Get to the point.'

'I was awarded a bursary after winning the Free State Mathematics Olympiad when I was in matric. It paid for my lectures and the hostel during the first year, but I had to work evenings and weekends at the Spur for money to live on. The tips weren't great, but I managed. Then in my second year I had to pay the fees myself, something I couldn't manage on the tips from the Spur. There were many other jobs after that. I've even been a barman at the Sand du Plessis Theatre. I'd attend my lectures during the day and at night and on the weekends I'd work. At the start of this year I worked at the bar at the Southern Sun Hotel, the one we went to. And that's where I met Anthony. He went there whenever he had to meet clients he couldn't see at the club. And when he heard I study Accountancy . . . he later offered me the job of doing the books. And eventually also to sit at reception every night and close up afterwards. Taking bookings. If it wasn't for this money I couldn't finish my studies, get it? But . . . but the things I have seen over the past year . . . weren't always pleasant.'

He sighs and gets up. Engela wonders why he's pacing up and down the room. 'Like this thing with you. Them keeping you locked up and all. It's not right. I was thinking I should help you. Help you escape. But I don't know how, Sammy-Jo. I really don't know how. I can't just open the door and let you go. George is fine, but Anthony and Steve . . . those guys are real bad. They'll kill me . . .'

'For how long do you still have to work here?'

'Not for that much longer. End of February I'm out of here. I have a job already.'

The phone rings at reception. He goes to answer it, but turns at the door: 'Your turn after this. Your story. And I want to know everything.'

Engela can hear him answering the phone. No, the club is closed on Saturdays, she can hear him say. And no, there isn't a girl here that can be booked for tonight. Thanks, Jacques, thanks, she whispers. She goes to the toilet again and stops at the bar on the way back. She finds Jacques on the seat in front of the mirror again. 'This round's on me,' she giggles.

'Yes, yes, you joker. But I can't be drinking that much. Those first four have already gone to my head.'

Engela puts her glass down on the bedside table and stands in front of him. 'Jacques, after hearing my story you will need an entire bottle of brandy. That I promise you . . .'

Fifteen

Thursday, 23 December 1993

It's quiet inside the club this morning and I haven't got anything to do. I don't feel like drinking for a change and now I'm lying here on my bed and writing in my diary. What will happen to this diary one day, I often wonder. Will someone read it one day? Will I ever get out of here? How I'm going to get through the next twelve days I really don't know. We had our last clients last night and then the club closed. It's only reopening next year. On Tuesday, 4 January, that's when they will be back, is what Jacky and Nadia said last night before the taxi came to pick them up. They were in good spirits because they made a lot of money this week, even though they only worked three nights. The guys enjoy blowing their Christmas bonuses, Jacky joked. I've noticed the last two weeks Jacques gets me fewer and fewer bookings. And he books more clients with Jacky and Nadia and the other girls that come work here for a night or two or maybe three. It doesn't bother me because I think I have hidden enough money to have a good life for quite some time.

Funny, when Jacky and Nadia left last night I thought about how I would miss them. They both kissed me good-bye on my cheek and wished me a Merry Christmas. George is going to the coast, I heard, and Anthony is off to China. Steve will also be gone, but I don't know where he's going. It's only me staying behind. Jacques is also going away, he said, but only for New Year. He and friends of his are going to hike in the Drakensberg. He promised to bring me a whole lot of books and videos to pass the time. It seems the bosses trust him enough to leave the keys with him, because he has to come in over the season to bring me food. On Tuesday I asked Anthony again if I couldn't go. I have been working here for two months and he promised it will only be a while before I can go. But then he said I was too big an asset for the club and that he couldn't let me go right now. I took a chance and told him I was happy here and that I enjoyed my work and that I just wanted to go home for Christmas and then I'd come back, but he just said he didn't believe me. George put a cold pudding in the refrigerator yesterday. He said I should have it on Christmas day.

*   *   *

Engela closes her diary and puts it down on the bedside table. She puts her new Parker pen away in the plastic holder lined with black fabric. She's never had such a smart pen, she told Jacques excitedly last week when he gave it to her wrapped in paper.

She strolls to the kitchen and makes herself a sandwich and a cup of coffee. She suddenly feels like a home-cooked meal – the meat stews Aunt Susan would make on a Sunday, or the chops Uncle Joshua sometimes grilled. Why has no one come looking for her? Is she just nobody, someone everyone has forgotten? Have they all forgotten her name? The clock in the bar slowly ticks. It is one o'clock in the afternoon, she notices. Twelve days. That's how long she has to stay here on her own, and today is only day one. But then it's also twelve days of rest with no sweaty bodies pumping into her for R125 commission. Anthony left her 12 pills in the bar. One for each day. Also a packet of sleeping pills and three boxes of Panado. She walks to the TV room with her coffee and sandwich and switches on the Telefunken. On TV1, Gé Korsten is singing in front of a canal in Venice. She hates his music; why can't they play something decent? Deep Purple, or something like that. She switches to TV4 and watches ten minutes of *The Cosby Show*, but the wholesomeness of the Huxtable family starts to annoy her. She switches off the TV and leaves her empty plate and cup in the kitchen sink. She paces up and down in the club. Now what? What the hell is there to do to pass the time? She opens the kitchen drawer, presses a sleeping tablet from the foil wrapper and drinks it down with neat whisky. At least it will let her pass out, she knows. And let the day pass . . .

*   *   *

Engela is five years old. Her tracksuit is soiled and the jacket is torn at the back. Along with her brother and sister, she crawls between the seven lemon trees in the back yard looking for lemons that have fallen to the ground. Their parents are having an afternoon nap because the drinking started early today, but now the children are thirsty. There is no cordial in the house. When Dorothy wakes up later she will boil them cabbage for dinner, just like she does every evening.

The three children start to peel the twelve bright-yellow lemons they have collected. The fresh smell of the fruit fills the kitchen. They press the juice into a plastic container and mix it with water and sugar before pouring themselves a glass each. Somewhere a distant choir sings: 'Mary's Boy Child . . .'

Engela swings her legs under the table and wonders who is singing so sweetly. Then a lady sings. She is getting closer. Slowly Engela floats from her chair to the ceiling. When she looks down she sees her brother and sister drinking their lemon juice. The lady singing is right next to her. She takes her hand and pulls her through the roof, from where they fly far away into the dark night. The lady sings of angels and a king born on Christmas day. The most wonderful food aromas surround Engela. I also want some, I'm hungry, Engela moans and turns in her sleep. The choir sings louder now. 'Mum! I'm hungry!' Engela shouts and wakes herself up. Dream and reality mingle for a few seconds, but the lady's voice continues with the singing. In the distance Engela notices shepherds herding their sheep. A star shoots through the dark night. The light shoots all the way into her room and travels across her face. She sits up and rubs her eyes. The music is still playing but from somewhere in the club.

Engela's hair and tracksuit are rumpled from her afternoon nap when she gets up and walks towards the music. It's dark inside the bar, but a faint light is coming from the reception area. Then she sees Jacques sitting on the two-seater couch. Two candles are burning on the small table in front of him and another three on the desk. The final bars of Boney M's 'Mary's Boy Child' come from his cassette player. Jacques gets up and presses the white stop button without saying a word. Engela notices the two champagne glasses and the bottle of Boschen-dal Brut on the desk. The smell of hot pizza is coming from the two Toni's Pizza takeaway boxes. Pop! goes the cork. Jacques fills the glasses and hands one to Engela.

'Merry Christmas,' he says and clinks his glass against hers. Behind his head the candles create moving Christmas decorations against the walls.

'Merry Christmas,' she says.

'Christmas should really be a family affair,' Jacques says. 'But we don't have family to be with tonight, so we can only wish each other a Merry Christmas.'

Engela doesn't fight the salty tears running from her eyes. 'Come, sit down,' Jacques says. 'Hope you like pizza.' He presses the green play button on the cassette player and pulls his office chair closer to the table with the pizza. 'Enjoy.'

Engela smiles. 'Thank you, Jacques.'

'You have never told me what happened exactly the day your mother died.'

'Why do you want to know about all those things?' she asks through bites of pizza. 'She's dead.'

'Because I want to. Because I also lost a mother. That's why.'

She gets up and runs to her bedroom, scratches in her suitcase and returns with her diary. She turns to the beginning of the year and hands him the diary. 'There, read it yourself. I wrote it shortly after she died. Can't remember exactly when.' She points with her finger to the top of the page. 'I also didn't add a date. Don't know why. But you read it.'

*　　*　　*

The day starts like any other morning. Rushing to get ready for school, grabbing an apple or sandwich for the road and checking if I made my bed before closing my bedroom door. I run down the passage to her bedroom and knock gently. She lets me in and I find her sitting on the corner of the bed. I look around the room for my stepdad, kiss her on the forehead and tell her I love her. She grabs my hand and with tears in her eyes tells me the two of us will be starting a new life soon. I run out the front door and the gate. On my way to school I start mulling over the things Mummy told me the day before. She was waiting for me when I got back from school and called me into her bedroom straight away. I immediately noticed the letters on her bed, letters that had gone stale, letters that were read over and over again, letters that were sent years ago. She started telling me she was bitterly unhappy in her marriage. She started telling me about her life as a child, her dreams, her future and what she hoped to achieve. This woman sitting in front of me was like a teenager sharing her deepest fantasies with me. She told me about her life before me and my siblings, her loves, the one big love of her life and how my father became part of her life. She told me how much she loved us, her children, how unhappy she was through all the years because she could never give us what we wanted and that alcohol had taken over her life. We laughed together, cried together, and I wiped her tears. I read letters exchanged between her and someone who once occupied a very special place in her life. It was love from a distance and a love both their parents didn't want for their children and so they had to give it all up and follow their own paths. It was a love that for years was kept strong through letters only. On that day I saw someone different who was more profound than my mother. I saw someone who was also a human being, somebody who could also love, somebody who regretted so many things, somebody who I could look up to just for that day. She was

148

my mother, she was the one who brought us into this mixed-up world and made it even more mixed-up, but who wanted many things to be different.

I have an Afrikaans lesson just after ten and I've left one of my books at home. My teacher tells me to run home quickly and fetch it. As I open the classroom door the bell goes and it's the next class. Relieved I turn around and grab my school bag from my desk. After school I walk home. As I approach the front door I notice my bedroom windows are closed. I am convinced that I opened them both before I left for school this morning. I wait at the front door, knock and call out to my mother to come open up. It's completely quiet inside the house. I walk around the house to the back door and try to open it. I call out to my mother but nothing happens. I go back to the front door and pull at it. I call out to my mother as loudly as I can, but she doesn't answer. I go back to my bedroom windows and out of the corner of my eye I notice one of my mother's bedroom windows are open. I look up through the window and notice something like blood against the curtains. I immediately start pushing a big drum towards the window so I can get on top of it to and look into her bedroom. I wiggle the window's hinge to open it wider. When I pull the curtains away I notice the pistol on the corner of the bed first. My eyes shift downwards and I see her, on the carpet, her body kind of pushed under the bed with the frill pulled up, as if somebody had actually pushed her under the bed, lifted the frill and then left her like that. I notice her eyes are open, staring at me. Her arms are outstretched on either side of her body, the palms of her hands are purple. 'Mummy . . . Mummy . . . it's me . . . open the door.' I jerk at the curtain and notice that it's covered in blood from top to bottom. I strain my head deeper through the window for a clearer view and then I see the blood-soaked towel on top of her chest. Her eyes keep staring at me, but she doesn't move at all. 'Mummy, it's me . . . get up . . . unlock the door for me.' Only then I realise what's going on. I jump off the drum and run to our neighbours. Those few minutes seemed like years to me. From the moment the police arrived, and the ambulance, and the doctor injected me, everything was like a dream.

I don't remember much from after I found her. But I do remember the doctor holding my hand while injecting me and looking me straight in the eye, telling me my mother was dead. I remember the police whispering . . . suicide . . . I remember the sounds of sirens and I remember seeing black in front of me.

*　*　*

'Wow, Sammy-Jo. That's rough,' Jacques says as he closes the diary. 'I didn't know you . . . you found her.' She doesn't respond. Later, he throws away the pizza boxes in the kitchen and refills their glasses. Engela lies stretched out on the couch, her hands under her head. Jacques sits down on the office chair again.

'Why are the police not doing anything, hey?' she wants to know as she stares at the ceiling.

'What do you mean?'

'This place. Why don't they come and arrest the bosses and break this place down? Then I'll be free. It just seems like . . . like nobody wants to do anything.'

'And why would they do that?' he counters. 'The police couldn't be bothered by prostitution. You should see what it looks like at the square and down towards the station. There the girls are standing next to the road waiting to get picked up. Over the past five years sex agencies have opened up all over the city. The police don't give a damn. And Anthony . . . on the surface he and his partners aren't doing anything wrong, so everyone's happy. Lady Femmé is a club like any other. Because no one knows you're being held against your will. Or about their smuggling business.'

'What are they smuggling?'

'That I don't know everything about. You pick up things along the way, or hear about something, you see the people arriving and disappearing with the bosses into the office at the back. That door is permanently locked. I have only been in there on a few occasions when I had to take them drinks. And before I enter I have to knock three times. Once there was a huge brief-case on the table. Anthony closed it quickly, but I saw it was stacked with money. One of the guys left a little later with the briefcase. But you soon learn not to ask questions. I suspect they smuggle big time. The club is only a smokescreen, if you ask me.'

'But what about all the girls? Surely that's wrong?'

'Nadia and Jacky are here of their own free will, Sammy-Jo. That much you know. They get on that bus in Johannesburg all by themselves every week to come work here. That's how things are. But you . . . in your case it's different. You are underage and held against your will. And that's against the law. That's why you're not allowed to speak to the clients. That's why you have to tell everyone you are twenty-one. Because nobody must know about you and your circumstances . . .'

'Cigarette?' Engela asks.

'Why not.'

'I'll go get.' Engela goes to the bar where an open packet of

Benson & Hedges sits on the counter. She lights one for each of them.

'I have wondered sometimes . . . these girls coming to work here on a Thursday and Friday, I get the feeling they are also not doing it out of their own free will,' Jacques continues. 'They are dropped here and picked up again later. Have you noticed they don't talk to anyone?'

'Because they can't speak English or Afrikaans.'

Jacques laughs. 'Yes, they are usually Chinese. George once told me they work at all the clubs from Klerksdorp down to here. A different place every night. I also think that . . . judging by their behaviour, they are also being kept by their owners and rented out to the various clubs. That's what I think. Some of them also seem pretty young to me. Those girls . . . Anthony doesn't pay them per client, did you know that? He pays a fixed amount upfront to the guy bringing them. The more clients they manage, the better for the club.'

'How am I going to get out of here, Jacques? I don't think the bosses are planning on ever letting me go.'

He looks at her for a long time before he speaks. 'I'll get you out of here, Sammy-Jo. I promise. Since you told me . . . it's all I think about.'

'But how? Unlock the door so I can go!'

'You know I can't do that. They will know it was me and then I will never be safe again. Or be able to work. Anthony threatened me once. Said if ever I got him into trouble he would see to it that not a single accounting firm in the country ever hired me.'

'And how would he manage that?'

'Easy. There are many ways. An anonymous call, for example, with a little hint: "That Jacques dude who started with you recently, did you know he was involved with money laundering?"

Something like that. In any case, it would be too dangerous for you to escape. They will be worried you might talk, so they will come looking for you.'

'But what am I going to do?'

Jacques weighs his words carefully. 'I'll get you out of here . . . I just have to get the plans in order.'

'Like what?'

'It would have to happen in such a way that no one can point a finger at me, but also that you will be safe and fine for the rest of your life—'

Engela suddenly sits up straight. 'Really? When?'

'Wait, Sammy-Jo, wait. I'm not a pro at these things. Give me a chance.'

Chance's arse, Engela thinks. She blows tiny smoke rings in front of her. Jacques won't do anything. Next year he leaves and she stays behind. She'll have to make her own plans. The cassette player clicks when the cassette finishes.

'Trust me, Sammy-Jo. Just trust me.'

'Can I . . . call my dad, Jacques?' she asks after a while.

'Sammy-Jo, why do you make it so difficult for me?'

'Please!'

'You know the club telephone is locked. No one can make calls when the bosses aren't around. You know that.'

'There are telephone booths on the square.'

'I don't know. Geez, I don't know.'

'Jacques? Please?'

*　*　*

Hoffman Square is deserted when Jacques parks in front of the post office at ten that evening. Even the buses aren't running, because the daily commuters are now either somewhere far away on holiday or with family on Christmas Eve.

'Don't sound scared. Don't cry. Don't let slip anything. Please, Sammy-Jo.' He hands her a bunch of coins. She inserts three 50-cent coins into the slot and dials her dad's home number. It rings for quite a while before he picks up in a sleepy voice. 'Andries, good evening.' Engela wants to say something, but the words get stuck inside her mouth. She swallows a few times. 'Hi, Dad . . . it's me . . . Engela,' she finally says.

*   *   *

Saturday, 25 December 1993

And so Christmas arrived. My dad said that Barry and Miems would be visiting him and Auntie Susan today.

I told him I was okay and that they shouldn't worry about me. My dad wanted to know where I was, but I assured him I was safe. I had to apply all my willpower to remain strong. I wanted my dad to cause a scene, I expected a police car any second to come and save me . . . I wanted to be saved, but nothing happened . . . Nothing happened, no flyers were handed out on the streets, no policemen looking for me door to door. I was satisfied because I had talked to him, if only I could tell him what was really going on. I knew if I said something life would become very difficult for me. It was a very awkward conversation, my dad was quiet as always and I didn't add anything. We drove back to the club and my heart was broken. Couldn't he hear the pain in my voice and that something was wrong? I cried in my heart, but didn't shed a tear. At the club Jacques said his good-byes and locked everything.

And now I'm going to eat the cold pudding George left in the refrigerator for me. It's Christmas.

Sixteen

Nadia, Jacky and Engela are sitting and chatting merrily at the bar counter while the three club owners are meeting in the office behind the locked wooden door. Nadia has to answer the phone because Jacques hasn't turned up for work. Maybe he'll be back tomorrow night, Engela hopes quietly. The three girls are appropriately made-up and skimpily dressed, as is required, ready for their clients. But tonight the club doors, and their clients' wallets, remain firmly closed.

'I said it was silly to reopen so early in the year,' Jacky complains. 'But they wouldn't listen now, would they? I mean, it's only the fourth today. Everybody's still on holiday. We could have stayed home. You'll see. If we have any clients at all this week, it will be one at a time. And few and far between.'

'Was the same thing last year,' Nadia continues. 'But overall January is usually a quiet month. All the daddies spending their rands on the mummies, and now they're broke and there's nothing left for us!'

'Shame on them!'

The telephone rings and Nadia gets up to answer it.

'Goodness, Sammy-Jo. It's really nice seeing you again,' Jacky says happily. 'I missed you a little, you know.'

'No, he's not available at the moment, but give me your number and he'll call you back,' Engela and Jacky can hear Nadia say.

'What did you do all the time?' Jacky wants to know.

'Oh, I slept, watched TV, read books, wrote in my diary, and slept, drank and slept again. And drank a little bit more,' Engela giggles. She doesn't say a word about the time she and Jacques spent together.

The call was for Anthony, urgent, apparently, Nadia explains as she passes them on her way to the office. She knocks three times, waits for the door to be opened and hands the note with the message to Anthony. Funny, she thinks. No one ever phones Anthony on the club number at reception. That number is strictly for clients looking for pleasure; the club owners have their own telephone in the office, a number known to only a select few of their business associates.

'Oh well, here we are, the three of us again, right?' she says when she returns to the bar. She frowns, as if she's just had the brightest idea ever. 'Sammy-Jo, tell you what. Since I have to man the phone and the front door, and George is still busy in the office, you'll have to substitute and play barlady and see to it that our glasses are never empty. How does that sound?'

'Fine by me,' Engela responds happily and gets to the task immediately. Heaven knows, she's glad they're back. The days just got too long and too lonely. But . . . where could Jacques be? Three days after Christmas he brought fresh salads, bread and canned food before he and his buddies went hiking in the Drakensberg, but he said he would be back the day before yesterday already and that he would come and check if she was okay straight away. He didn't. Has he now also dropped her?

'You're a jolly bunch,' Steve says when he enters the bar after an hour to pour himself and the other two some drinks. 'But it's not going to pay the bills. No calls or bookings, Nadia?'

Nadia shakes her head. 'It's too early in the month, Steve. You know there's no business in the first week of January.'

'They will come. We're running a big advertisement in tomorrow's *Volksblad*. Half price entrance until Friday. Not everyone can be away or broke, surely.' And then, as an afterthought: 'It's costing us a lot of money, the special. But we're doing it for you, you know?'

The girls don't say anything, but Nadia and Jacky nod their heads in appreciation. Yes, they know.

'Nadia, we'd like to see you in the office. Come round in half an hour.'

When Steve is gone the three women look at each other with wide eyes. When the bosses want to see someone in the office there is big trouble. Very big trouble, they know. 'I hope I don't get fired,' Nadia says with a worried look on her face. She pushes her empty glass over to Engela. 'Make it a triple, just to play safe.'

Jacky lays a protective hand on Nadia's arm. 'Nadia, just remember: mercy is always bigger than the problem.'

Nadia looks at her colleague in surprise. 'Hell, Jacky, that's deep. Where do you get this shit?'

'Read it somewhere during the holidays. On the back of a sugar sachet.' Jacky doesn't really understand what it means, but because it sounded cool she memorised the words so she could use it again. And this situation was appropriate, she thought. The telephone rings again.

'It's ten o'clock, girls. Do you feel like a client? Not me,' Nadia says as she gets up to answer the phone. The other two shake their heads. No, they also don't feel like it. Tomorrow is another day. Tonight is a chance for the three of them to have a good time. 'Sorry, dear,' they hear Nadia saying on the phone. 'We are fully booked tonight, but what about tomorrow night?'

Jacky clicks her fingers like a naughty child. 'Shit, if the bosses had to hear that.'

Engela keeps topping up their glasses and Nadia checks the time on the clock on the wall. Exactly thirty minutes after Steve's command she gets up. 'Wish me luck, girls,' she says and goes down the passage.

Her conversation with the three men in the office lasts only seven minutes, and then she returns to the bar. 'Do tell!' Jacky encourages her.

'Three things. First of all – I didn't get fired.'

'Yes, and?'

'We're done for the night, we can go to our rooms. The bosses are leaving in ten minutes. Then we're alone.' She winks naughtily. 'And then, my dear friends, we go big!'

'And the third thing?'

'As of tomorrow I have to play receptionist for the rest of the month when Anthony is busy. Otherwise he will be helping out.'

Engela feels a shiver run down her spine and goose bumps on her skin. She puts her glass down on the bar counter, shaking slightly. Something's not right . . . it just doesn't make sense. 'But why?' she wants to know. 'Where is Jacques?'

Nadia answers her without hesitation: 'He fell or something. Three days ago. Somewhere in the mountains.'

'Fell?'

'Yes, he fell. That's all Anthony said. Now I have to substitute for him. That call just now, the message, apparently it was from the hospital in Harrismith.'

'Nadia!' Jacky calls out in shock. 'Shit, man, how did it happen?'

'Don't know. I told you Anthony didn't say much more, and I didn't want to ask straight away. We'll probably know later.'

'When . . . when will he . . . come back, Nadia?' Engela asks.

Nadia rubs her head. 'Pour us another one first, dear.'

Engela jumps up and slaps her hand on the bar counter. 'No! When, Nadia? When is he coming back?'

Nadia looks at Engela standing in front of her in a rage. Her childlike eyes stare at Nadia as if it's her fault. 'Sammy-Jo, relax—'

'Relax my arse, Nadia! When is he coming back?'

'Well, Anthony said . . . he said . . . maybe never again. The accident was serious . . . very serious, that's what the hospital said.'

A few seconds pass in absolute silence. Maybe three, or even five. Maybe even more. In moments like these it seems as if time stands still. As if time and words don't exist. That everything is so final nothing exists. As if life itself doesn't exist, because all hope was erased with a few words. Maybe never again, Nadia said.

Then Engela screams. Raw, animal sounds escape from her. The intensity of it shatters the last fragments of what remains of her heart. The shards rage through her lungs and surge up her throat before bursting out of her mouth. 'No! No! Nooooo!' She grabs her glass and throws it at the shelves in front of her. Bottles tumble down and shatter on the tiled floor. 'No!' She kicks over the bar-stool she was sitting on, and then the next one. 'No! Not this! Jacques!' She grabs Jacky's glass. More bottles fall to the floor.

The three partners come storming from the office. 'What the hell is going on here?' Anthony shouts.

George grabs Engela by the arm, but she breaks loose and slaps his face. 'Fuck you! Fuck all of you!' She topples two more bar-stools on her way to her bedroom. She slams the door with force behind her. 'No! No! No!' the yelling reverberates from behind the closed bedroom door. Nadia and Jacky look at each other in bewilderment; something must have happened during the holidays, something between Jacques and Sammy-Jo, they know instinctively. That's the only time a woman goes hysterical like that. Steve is on his way to the bedroom to sort her out.

'Steve!' He freezes in his tracks. He has never heard Jacky speak in that tone. 'Leave it. Steve! Just leave it! She's had too much to drink. She'll be fine tomorrow.'

For a second he's not sure what to do next. 'Yes, fine,' he says angrily. 'But you better see to it that she doesn't lose it like that again. Just look at the mess in the bar.'

'Tsk, tsk,' Anthony clicks his tongue. 'This is big damage. Pity we'll have to deduct it from her commission. What a shame.'

*   *   *

The advertisement in the newspaper must have helped; by nine o'clock five clients have already rung the doorbell. Steve takes over from Nadia at reception so that she can also provide room service; George is back behind the bar and Anthony cleans glasses and ashtrays.

Damn Jacques, he thinks, annoyed.

Everything around Engela occurs in a daze. Following her outburst last night and her refusal this morning to do any more work, Steve ordered Jacky to keep her on a steady dose of tranquillisers. Jacky and Nadia are in high spirits under the caressing hands of four clients as they chat next to the bar counter. The two girls have already agreed: two guys each, and they are going to convince them very soon to continue the party in the room with the double bed. Four wallets will be paying for the same hour's work.

'Come on, guys, I am starving for a proper group session!' Nadia sets the ball in motion.

The guys like what they're hearing. 'I'm in!' one of them says. 'And you?' The others agree laughingly.

Out of the corner of her eye Nadia notices the fifth client still sitting at the bar nursing his beer. Okay, he's out for now. She indicates to George that they're off to the room. He nods his head. 'Another beer?' he asks the quiet guy across from him.

'No, thanks, I'm okay.' He offers his hand to George. 'Hi, I'm Ian. It's my first time tonight with you guys.'

'I know. We know our clients. Anyway, welcome, Ian, welcome.'

'Thanks.'

'Hope you'll have a good time and that we'll be seeing you often.'

Ian leans over to George. 'The girl over there, is she available?'

'Yes, she is. And she's good, hey, very good. The guys just love her.'

'Excellent,' Ian says. 'Do they travel?'

'Yes, but then it's a little more expensive. Why do you ask?'

'Because if she's as good as you say I would like her to come over tomorrow evening.'

'No problem, Ian, no problem. Where are you staying?'

'At a hotel. The Southern Sun. It's in—'

'In Brandwag,' George interrupts him. 'I know. We do business over there regularly. No problem. Come, let me introduce you.'

The men go up to Engela, who is staring into space.

'Sammy-Jo, meet Ian.'

'Hi' is all she says when the new client sits down next to her. George leaves them alone.

'Did you check him out?' Steve whispers to George when he's back behind the counter.

'Yes, he's fine, one of those quiet types, you know.'

They keep an eye on Ian and Sammy-Jo when the two get up a little later and go to the back. Engela passes the room where Jacky and Nadia are busy doubling their hourly income. She goes to one of the single rooms with a massage table. Ian follows her. She wants to get this over with as quickly as possible. No chitchat and fooling around. Just before Ian enters the room he looks back and notices Steve standing at the end of the passage. He quickly closes the door behind him and bolts it. Engela undresses in a hurry, throws her clothes down on the floor and gets up on the massage table, naked. Instinctively and without showing any emotion she opens her legs. Just let it be over and done with quickly, please, she prays. She doesn't have the energy for this tonight. What the hell really happened to Jacques? Outside in the passage Steve walks up to the door.

'Suck it, baby, suck it!' he hears Ian shouting. And Sammy-Jo screaming. The quiet guy turned out not to be so quiet after all, Steve thinks as he walks back to the bar. Still waters run deep, that's what they always say.

It isn't over that quickly, and it's an hour before Ian and Engela return from the room. Engela goes back to her spot at the bar, but Ian walks straight to the reception area. She sees him talking to Steve, who writes something in the book on Jacques' desk.

'You okay?' George asks. She just nods her head. Then Jacky and Nadia appear noisily with their four benefactors. The new year hasn't got off to such a bad start after all.

'Cheers,' the three business partners drink to each other in the office later that evening. 'To a prosperous 1994.'

The girls go to their rooms when the club's doors close.

Steve starts laughing. 'That guy who booked Sammy-Jo, Geez, that dude is a flipping weirdo. You won't believe me!'

'He seemed a little strange to me also,' says George.

'In the bar he seemed out of place at first, but when they went to the room, he suddenly became a tiger. I heard him through the door shouting at Sammy-Jo. And afterwards he booked her again for tomorrow night. At the Southern. With the strangest request . . . wait for this one.'

'Yes, we're listening?'

Steve can't control his laughter. 'She has to . . . she has to . . . tie her hair in a ponytail and take a teddy bear with!'

Anthony shakes his head. 'Yes, there are some sick people out there.'

Seventeen

'Sammy-Jo, are you almost ready to go?' Steve calls out the following afternoon, just after five o'clock, before entering her bedroom without knocking. She is sitting in front of the mirror holding a make-up brush in one hand. Her hair is combed tightly back and tied in a ponytail. The black coat and the teddy bear he bought her that morning are lying on the bed.

'Almost done,' she says.

'Do you want a drink before we go?'

'No, I'm fine.'

'Good. See you in twenty minutes. And don't be late. Ian said I should have you there at exactly six o'clock.'

She nods without saying a word. When he closes the door she adds the final touches to her face, puts her coat on and looks at herself in the mirror. Everything looks fine. She throws over her shoulder the handbag she packed earlier in the afternoon and presses the teddy bear against her.

'We can go,' she tells Steve in the bar.

The sun is low and shining from ahead as they drive in the direction of Brandwag.

'Sammy-Jo—'

'Yes, I know,' she interrupts him. 'Don't try anything funny.'

'Just checking that you know.'

'I've been to the hotel before, remember. Did I try anything funny then?'

Steve doesn't respond. A porter comes running when he stops in the parking area in front of the hotel, but Steve gestures that they're all right.

'I take you to the room. From there you're on your own. I'll be waiting—'

'. . . downstairs in the bar,' Engela finishes his sentence. 'And I know the bar has an unrestricted view of the lobby and you check everyone leaving so I won't be able to run away, and in an hour you will come and fetch me from the room.'

Steve grins. 'I see Jacques has educated you nicely, Sammy-Jo. Well done.'

The lobby is swarming with holiday-makers checking in for the night before continuing homeward in the morning – either north or south. Steve's eyes scan the room allocation board on the wall, but then Ian suddenly appears behind them. 'It's okay, she can come with me.' He nods in approval as he looks at Engela standing in front of him, dressed in the black coat and clutching the teddy bear. 'I'm happy to see you can . . . how shall I put it . . . fulfil a man's . . . needs.' He puts his hand out to Engela. 'Come, Sammy-Jo, let's not waste any time.'

Steve stops him. 'I have to escort her to the room. It's our rules.'

A waiter dressed in a black suit stands motionless against a pillar five paces behind them, balancing a silver tray in his hand. Stony-faced, he observes Steve, Engela and Ian.

'As you like,' says Ian, turning on his heels and leading the way. 'Follow me.' His room is the first one in the first corridor that extends to the right coming out of the lobby. Room 101. Ian pushes the door open. 'You'll fetch her in an hour, right?' he confirms with Steve. He doesn't wait for an answer, but leads Engela into the room. When Steve hears the door being locked he turns and goes to the bar. He orders a Lion and chooses a seat with a clear view of the busy lobby. Porters with trolleys are running up and down between guests queuing up to check in. Geez, why did this guy have to choose such a busy time for his appointment . . .? He must remember to go and see Pieter, he thinks after a while. Just to thank him for introducing Sammy-Jo to them. She brings in the most money for the club, yet they pay her less commission than the others. But nobody has to know that. She will have to work at least another year, they decided at their meeting last night.

'Is there a Mr Steve Grand in the bar?' Steve jumps in surprise when, after just fifteen minutes, a black-suited waiter suddenly calls out his name. The waiter carries a silver tray. 'Steve Grand? Are you here?' Everyone in the bar looks first at the waiter and then all around them. 'Mr Grand?'

Steve lifts his hand instinctively and stands up. 'Yes, why?' he asks warily when the waiter walks up to him.

'Sorry to disturb you, sir,' the man whispers to Steve. He looks at the note on the tray. 'You are Mr Grand?'

'Yes.'

'Mr Steve Grand?'

'That's what I said. Yes.'

'Sorry to disturb you, sir.'

'Yes, yes, that's fine. Why are you looking for me?'

'Sir, there is a phone call for you at reception.'

'Impossible. Nobody knows I'm—' Steve cuts himself off just in time.

'Apparently it is very urgent, sir. Once again, sorry for disturbing you, sir.'

Steve shakes his head. 'It can't be. It must be a mistake.' The guests at the bar resume their conversations. Steve peeps over the waiter's shoulder to the lobby, where the noise is increasing as hotel guests arrive and gather in front of the reception desk.

'No, sir, it's no mistake.' The waiter once again stares at the note on the tray. 'You are Steve Grand, right?'

Steve is getting irritated by the man's persistence.

'Yes! That's what I said! And no, I'm not expecting any bloody phone calls!

'What's your room number, sir?'

'Just leave me alone!'

'Sorry, sir, sorry. Don't shoot the messenger.' He gives Steve a broad smile. 'You are sure that you are Mr Steve Grand, right? And I am sure there is a phone call waiting for you. Right. But . . .' He looks at his watch. 'It is now already four minutes later . . . and, sir, the guy looking for you . . . is—'

'I fucking told you! I don't expect any phone calls!' Steve is about to smack him, but then he realises everyone in the bar is watching them.

The waiter holds the tray protectively in front of him and stands back half a pace. 'Sorry, sir, but don't shoot the messenger.'

'Relax, dude. It's still the holiday season,' somebody shouts behind Steve. He turns swiftly. This guy wants a smack.

'Keep your nose out of my business, okay?' When Steve turns back the waiter has disappeared among the hotel guests. It's strange, very strange. Who would be calling him? Only his two partners know where he is. There is a coin-operated telephone on top of a glass pedestal in the corner of the bar. Steve inserts a 50-cent coin and dials the club's private number. No, Anthony says, they weren't looking for him. What's the matter?

Something's not right, Steve realises. He leaves the bar in a rush, pushing the people in the lobby aside, goes into the corridor and knocks on the door of room 101. No answer. He knocks harder. Still nothing. Back in the lobby, Steve pushes to the front of the reception desk. He is looking for his friend in 101, he tells the girl behind the desk, and could she please call him and ask him to meet Steve in the bar?

'Sure, sir. What's his surname?' she asks.

'It's Ian—' He stops himself.

'And his surname, sir?'

'It's . . . sorry . . . I don't know . . . but it's Ian, in room 101. It's urgent. Call him, now!'

The receptionist scans the computer screen in front of her. 'Sorry, sir, nobody has been booked into room 101.'

'That's impossible! I was there a while ago! I . . . I think I left my wallet in the room. Please just call, would you?'

'But there's no one there, sir.'

'Okay. Okay then. Just get someone to unlock for me so I can get my wallet.'

'You're not confusing the room number by any chance?'

Steve leans across the desk. His face goes red with anger. 'Go open that bloody door,' he hisses in her face. To avoid an unpleasant scene in front of the other guests, she smiles back at Steve. Let the arsehole go and see for himself. She calls a porter and hands him an access card.

But room 101 is empty. There's no one there. The long black coat and the teddy bear lie on the bed. Steve grabs the teddy bear. There is a long cut between the teddy bear's legs, he notices. He pushes his fingers inside. The teddy's stuffing has been removed.

*   *   *

'You can relax now. We're safe,' says Ian to the girl next to him in the car. The lights of Bloemfontein are thirty minutes behind them already. The N1 northbound is busy with holiday-makers driving the last 350 kilometres back to the Transvaal.

'Where are we going?' Engela asks. Hanging from the rear-view mirror is a plastic card with the words 'Nothing is impossible for God' printed on it.

'To a small town called Ladybrand. It's not very far. Another two hours or so. Soon we will turn off to Excelsior and then we're almost there. But we're taking the long route. The actual way from Bloem is through the city, then along the N8 past the airport. I thought it would be safer to avoid the city centre, Botshabelo and Thaba Nchu tonight.'

Engela is suddenly filled with doubt. Can it be true? Is she really free? Is this stranger next to her really her rescuer? What if he is just another abductor who has stolen her for his place? She trusted him straight away without thinking. 'You are genuine, aren't you?' she asks. 'You really have come to rescue me? I don't even know who you really are, but after last night I did everything exactly the way you instructed me to.'

'Ian. That's my real name. But I will understand if you don't trust me completely yet. Everything probably feels very unreal to you, right? I mean, the last twenty-four hours?'

'Yes, kind of. You gave me a big fright in the room last night when you shouted like that all of a sudden.'

'I'm sorry, I had to. Steve was outside in the passage and I had to do something so he wouldn't become suspicious. When you screamed on top of that . . . it was perfect.'

After that scream Ian had picked her clothes up from the floor and handed them to her. Get dressed, he ordered. She didn't expect this, but she obliged. That's what the club had taught her: you behave and you just do. He sat down next to her. You are Engela, right? He wanted to be certain. She was startled when she heard her name, but he pressed his finger against her lips and indicated that she should keep quiet. After that he explained to her over and over again what was going to happen and what she was expected to do. When their hour in the room was up he checked once again that she understood everything. Back in the bar, Engela noticed him talking to Steve to arrange her booking for the following evening, exactly the way he said he would. This morning Steve had brought her the big teddy bear and laughed as he said: 'Your funny client wants you to take this along tonight.' Along with the teddy bear came the black coat she had to wear. Engela didn't sleep and didn't drink anything today. When Steve went out she immediately made a cut at the bottom end of the teddy, removed the stuffing and hid it under her mattress. She rolled her money into small bundles and inserted them into the teddy bear. Her diary and a few personal items, like the pendant her mother bought her three years ago, she hid in the coat pockets and in her handbag. In the afternoon she made up her face a little and tied her hair high up in a ponytail behind her head. No hair could be visible underneath the wig. When Ian closed the hotel room door in Steve's face some time later they didn't talk much. She removed her money from the teddy bear and put it in the green sports bag on the table, along with all the other possessions she had brought. On a shelf in the wardrobe was a matching green school tracksuit and a curly black wig. Ian stood at the door the whole time, checking his watch. She knew she had only fifteen minutes and thirty seconds to get everything done. Come, Ian said when it was time, and grabbed her hand. The door to room 101 shut behind them. Moments later, a father and his teenage daughter, she with black, curly hair and wearing a green tracksuit, passed through the lobby on their way out of the hotel. At the opposite end of the busy reception area a furious Steve was having an argument in the bar with a very stubborn waiter. 'Yes! That's what I said! And no, I am not expecting any bloody phone calls!' he snapped.

*   *   *

Engela can feel something pulling at her arm. Sleepily, she sits up in the passenger seat.

'Wake up, Engela, wake up.'

'Huh?' She notices street lamps. They are driving slowly down the main street of a town. 'Where are we?'

'Ladybrand,' Ian says. 'We're here. Safely.'

'Really? Then . . . then it wasn't just another dream?'

'No, but a tough time lies ahead of you before you can be reunited with your father.'

Engela feels fear. 'Like what?'

'I didn't want to wake you while you were sleeping, but let's quickly discuss a few practical arrangements before we arrive at the Home.'

Nothing is impossible for God, declares the plastic card dangling from the rear-view mirror.

'Tonight you will eat and rest, that's all. At this very moment the police in Bloemfontein are conducting a raid on Lady Femmé. Tomorrow you will have to make a statement at the police station in town and tell them everything that has happened to you since October last year. They will probably interrogate you for at least four hours. After that we will go to Harrismith. To the hospital there. You will have to stay there for a few days. My sister is the matron at the hospital. They will do a complete medical check-up on you. And I believe you are also addicted to drugs and other medication. We will have to assist you with that. Otherwise, you are going to go through hell. So that's basically that. But we will need your cooperation.'

It's too much for Engela to process. 'Everything happened so quickly last night and today, but . . . I wanted to ask . . . how do you know all these things about me? How do you know me . . . and how did you find me?'

Ian laughs. 'Yes, my apologies, there probably wasn't enough time for the finer details. But I actually thought you would know.'

High above, in a flawless eastern Free State sky, a star shoots past. Ian drives through a white gate. Memorial Children's Home, Engela reads on the signboard against the wall. He and his wife are the houseparents, Ian says casually as he stops the car in front of a white building with a wide, open stoep. Yellow light bulbs are burning outside the front door. She gets out. Somebody approaches them from the side of the building, out of the darkness. Engela can't make out the face, but the outline looks familiar. She stops in surprise. Him? It can't be true? How is this possible?

'Hello, Engela,' Jacques says as he stands in front of her. 'I'm happy that you are safe now. Really happy.'

Part two
A new beginning

Free from drugs and alcohol

The first few days after my escape from the club I suffered terrible withdrawal symptoms: I was feverish, I hallucinated and threw up, every muscle in my body ached and I was often drenched in sweat. I wanted to get hold of drugs with all my might, even though I was given medication in the hospital to help me. I would sleep for hours on end, but as soon as I woke up I would cry all over again about the awful muscle aches, the headaches, the stomach aches, the aches in my wrists. I realised that withdrawal was the only way to drain the poison from my system. Even though great parts of this period in my life remain a complete blank, I will never forget the pain and loneliness I had to endure. What I do remember is that my nails and toenails were purple-blue; some of my toenails dropped off and my nails lifted. It was incredibly sore, but also part of the poison working itself out of my system. I had to wrestle with it, and for hours I would sit and stare at the ceiling of my room. Sometimes I would curl up again from the pain; sometimes my entire body itched. Then I would scratch my toes, my fingers, my neck, my stomach and, before I knew it, my entire body until they bled. I felt wretched; the entire experience was sheer hell and I became extremely thin. There were times when all I wanted to do was die. After some time I started to feel like a human again; I started eating, and bathed like a princess. My complexion returned to normal, and I was able to see my true self in the mirror. I wish I had the willpower these days that I had way back then . . . I still cannot believe I managed to get through it all. The symptoms didn't vanish overnight, and for some time I craved that floating feeling I got from the pills. I wanted to experience it again, I wanted to feel cold and unapproachable again, but I knew it would keep me in the prison of destruction. My life was shattered and I had to pick up the pieces again and overcome my addiction completely. Today I realise that I didn't go through it alone, but that I was carried all the way through by the power of God . . .

My path thereafter

When I was strong enough, I plucked up my courage and went back to Dewetsdorp. I will never forget the joy on my step-mother's face. Even though my dad was also happy to see me, there was a chilling distance between us. I moved into my old room. We never discussed what had happened, and slowly but surely I became more confident, determined to start a new life.

The police inquiry into my mother's death had been closed and finalised as a suicide, but a new detective in town went through her file again. Something wasn't right, he told me. I had to look at the photographs of the scene of her suicide again and tell him everything I could remember. He worked on the case for months on end, and I had to relive everything. There was enough evidence to prove that she did not in fact commit suicide, but not enough to prove that she was murdered. To this day I still do not know for sure what to believe or think about it. Suicide? Murder? I don't know. One of the worst things about her death I have to live with is that the inquiry determined that she lived for two to three hours after she was shot. The bullet entered the main artery in her neck and exited through her back. Apparently she was on her knees when she was shot, but it appears she got up afterwards, went to the bathroom, got a towel to press onto the wound and walked to the window to call for help. To my dismay, the inquiry determined that she drowned in her own blood. However, I have managed to come to terms with her death. At times, yes, it hurts very much when I start wondering again about what exactly happened that day. I really would like to know the truth, the truth about how her life ended, but will it be of any use to me? Will it make me a better person? She is resting now, and one day when I am with God the truth will be revealed.

I will remember her the way she was. I remember the morning of her death so well. She was sitting on the bed; I went to say goodbye to her, kissed her on the forehead and told her I loved her. I would rather cling to those memories than open old wounds that could lead to more pain and sorrow. She had many flaws and wasn't really a mother to us, but I long for her and miss her terribly. Sometimes I wish she could see me today, where I am, what I do. And sometimes I wonder what would have happened if she and I had indeed fled from my stepfather's house that afternoon. What would our lives be like today?

I never saw my stepdad again after my mother's death. My dad and brother have also passed away in the meantime. My brother and I never got the chance to talk about everything, but I believe he didn't know where I was. For a very long time I didn't have any contact with my sister, but fortunately she is part of my life again – a wonderful second chance for both of us.

I didn't go back to school and only have standard seven (grade nine). I left school midway through standard eight. I started work at the Dewetsdorp Hotel, where I literally did everything: receptionist, waitress, bar-girl and cleaner. But I wanted to get away, and jumped at the opportunity when I heard about a job at a hotel in Hoopstad. The owner and his wife came to fetch me, and that was where I continued my life. I worked long hours but enjoyed it thoroughly. I didn't want to look back on the past; I just wanted to continue on my own. I couldn't speak to people about my experiences at the time; I just wanted to forget. It also took me a long time to function normally. Emotionally, I was like a robot and followed the same routine every day: got up, took a bath, got ready for work and then went to the bar. When the bar closed at night I went back to my room and slept.

I had been there for a few weeks when I met the father of my daughter. We started going out and soon I moved in with him in Hoopstad – and fell pregnant. Michaela Christine Davis was born on 2 February 1998, after twenty-one hours of labour. Exactly two weeks after her birthday in 2013, her father died in a motorcycle accident. It took her a long time to process his death, something I totally understand. To this day she wishes she could have spent more time with him, but we can't predict life and we don't know what the future holds. As a mother I sometimes wish I could carry her pain, but support and love is all I can provide. I can tell her that Jesus loves her and that He sees her pain, and that I also don't know why certain things in life happen but that everything will be fine in the end.

'The day I held you for the first time everything stood still, my dear child. You were and still are my miracle. You were born from a body that was mutilated, you were formed inside me when I was still raw. You immediately crawled deep into my heart, you are the one who came to take my tears away and you are the hope I was praying for.'

After separating from her father, I moved to Bethal, where I got a job as an assistant at an auditing firm. I developed a love for book-keeping. It was also in Bethal that I would eventually meet my husband. He was from Johannesburg and worked at Mibco (Motor Industry Bargaining Council). For months on end, he would come visit me every weekend before I moved to Johannesburg. Today we live on a smallholding on the West Rand. I'm still a book-keeper. My greatest passion, however, is fighting for victims of human trafficking.

In 2012 I met the actor and motivational speaker Hykie Berg, a man whose heart is certainly in the right place. He is also the ambassador of PSARU (People Search and Rescue Unit). South Africans know him for his roles in TV series like *Plek van die Vleiseters*, *Egoli* and *Binnelanders*, and in films like *Forsaken* and *Rowwe Diamante*. These days he also testifies countrywide about being saved from the dark hell of drug addiction.

After our meeting, we started giving talks at churches, schools and other organisations. We also went to Dewetsdorp, among other places, to talk to the people there. That was a particularly special experience for me. When the two of us don't appear together, I travel a lot on my own to testify about my experiences and about the miracle of my salvation. To be rescued from the underworld where I was a sex slave, and then to overcome alcohol and drug addiction, is a miracle of God indeed.

The magazines *Finesse* (December 2012) and *Intiem* (January 2013), and radio stations like Radio Sonder Grense (RSG) and Radio Pulpit also provide me with the opportunity to tell my story through interviews. With the assistance of Karin and Flip Loots from Triple M Productions, the pharmacy chain Dis-Chem came on board in 2013 and sponsored a ten-minute video that was uploaded on YouTube and launched by *Rapport*.

Nicky Rheeder, one of the directors of the organisation Missing Children South Africa, contacted me in October 2013 to act as a public speaker for them. The TV personality Nico Panagio, famous as an actor on *Sewende Laan* and a presenter on *Top Billing*, is also a director of the organisation. He spends a lot of time locating missing children, particularly because the connection between human trafficking and missing children is so strong.

I have the highest respect for people like Hykie and Nico. They certainly don't feel superior because of their celebrity. They are people with heart and with the knowledge and means to reach out to all of society's lost, stolen and discarded souls. We need more people like them. We need more people to work with us and to pray with us. Everybody in South Africa should know what is happening in the dark underworld around us. As soon as possible.

A few cases

As I mentioned, my greatest passion these days is to create awareness of human trafficking and to locate missing children. People may think that human trafficking doesn't happen in South Africa, but it happens frequently. People also don't realise the connection between human trafficking and missing children. Did you know that every six hours a child goes missing in South Africa? That means nearly 1 460 children go missing every year.

Poverty plays one of the biggest roles in human trafficking. Parents sell their children to syndicates for as little as R250 because of promises of a better life and a huge income. But these parents know nothing about where their children go.

Rosettenville in Johannesburg is the area where human trafficking syndicates for the sex industry are probably the most active. The syndicates are, however, also active nationwide: from the port areas in every coastal city to small towns in the countryside. The young people we make contact with on the streets are often too scared to talk because they know their pimps are watching them. One false step and they know they will pay for it. On the streets we hear about the sadistic life that characterises human trafficking, and of children as young as ten years old appearing in pornographic videos. They are usually drugged so that they're unaware of what is happening to them. These pornographic videos are sold throughout South Africa.

Victims of human trafficking who are used in the sex industry bring in money for their 'owners' only for a while, because the clients always want fresh blood. The victims are therefore sold from one brothel to the next within a matter of months. Depending on client requirements, aspects like hair colour, build, nationality and race are considered. Victims are sometimes also sold at organised auctions, where a variety of buyers bid on them.

New victims are fed with drugs to make them dependent as quickly as possible, so that the owners can get a hold over them. They will never see healthy food. When their bodies become so gaunt that they literally are skin and bones, they are no longer of any use and are discarded. Many of these victims are never found – no traces or corpses are left behind.

Sometimes we do find a dead body, like that of a girl in a house in Johannesburg who was still chained up. According to the inquiry into her death, she had died of a drug overdose. We managed to locate her parents after an extensive search . . . but they didn't want to know anything about her.

The syndicates recruit their victims in many ways, but some of the more popular methods involve targeting solitary teenagers on streets or in shopping malls. That is why I always plead with parents not to drop their children off at shopping malls.

Another popular recruiting technique is to connect with teenagers on social media platforms. First a friendship is established, and then the attacker moves in. Recently I was involved with the case of a girl who was abducted just a few blocks from her house while she was walking to the shops. Her attacker had befriended her on Facebook. According to his false profile, he lived in Australia, but in fact he resided in the same neighbourhood as her. She came to trust him in such a short time that he knew exactly what she was doing, and where and when she would be alone. In this way he acquired useful information about when to pounce.

In another incident, one evening we found a heavily drugged twenty-year-old girl curled up on the pavement behind a low wall. We immediately had her admitted for medical treatment. She told us later that she had responded to an advertisement promising a good salary to part-time waitresses or hostesses at private functions. All they had to do was to carry drinks and mingle with the guests. Her first appointment was a disaster. She had to wear revealing clothes and drink with the businessmen. Her drink was spiked, however, and the men put money down on a table; the highest bidder could have her.

Part of my work is to place false advertisements regularly on various websites and platforms in order to lure syndicates, brothel owners and other sex offenders. Typically these advertisements will be something like 'Sexy teen looking for model contract' or 'Rich guy wants to have some fun'.

The responses to these advertisements are overwhelming, but we go through them patiently. As soon as we become suspicious we engage the person in conversation to gather as much information as possible, which we can hand over to the police at a later stage for their investigation. During one of these campaigns, where I was pretending to be a man, we got, among other things, the following feedback: 'I have a ten-year-old who is willing to have sex with you.'

Another case I will never forget happened quite recently in a small town in the countryside where I was giving a speech at the local church. A woman started talking to me afterwards. She was young and beautiful, but I could see that her soul was destroyed. She told me how her boyfriend would rent her out to sex syndicates so that he could repay his debts.

One night in 2012 I took a TV crew who wanted to see the world of human trafficking onto the streets of Johannesburg. As always, I wore a hat pulled low over my face so that no one would recognise me. I explained to the driver the way to a specific house I was acquainted with; I knew what was going to happen, but the TV crew did not. When we stopped in front of the house, armed men appeared as if from nowhere and walked towards us. The driver started to panic, but he followed my advice to drive off slowly and turn down the next street. Suddenly, behind us there were two or three vehicles with flashing lights that chased us out of the neighbourhood. This house was one of the many sex headquarters of syndicate leaders in Johannesburg. Their merchandise – the victims – comes not only from all over South Africa but also from other parts of Africa. When they receive new victims, the buyers are contacted to place their orders and to come and pick up their 'shopping'. Only then are vehicles allowed to park in front of the house. After the calls have been made and the transactions concluded, the cellphone SIM cards are destroyed. The armed guards who chased us from the area are paid thousands of rands every month to keep the syndicate leader safe.

I know how these guys go about their business; I have seen what they are looking for and how they make money. The victims mean nothing to them; they are focused only on the money they can make out of these poor people. On top of that, they think they are very powerful, but they are definitely not more powerful than God.

The statistics shock

Prostitution and sex trafficking are two different things and can't be judged in the same way. The two should also not be confused. Sex workers decide for themselves to earn an income from prostitution and nobody forces them into it. They can come and go as they like, or leave the industry altogether when they feel like it. Human trafficking in the sex industry is completely different. In this industry innocent teenagers are abducted, locked up, drugged and forced to have sex with clients. Human trafficking is when someone sells your body against your will to the sex industry. It reaches far beyond the sex industry, however – from organs being sold on the black market to slavery and offerings made during Satanic rituals. Human trafficking is exactly that: the buying and selling of human beings.

Do a Google search with words like 'human trafficking' or

'sex trafficking' and you will come across a vast array of articles on the subject. Here are a few examples:

Beeld, 20 June 2013

The nature of organised crime sometimes prohibits cases of prostitution, slavery and forced marriages involving underaged children to be reported.

Cases like that of a 14-year-old Angolan boy who was apparently used by a syndicate as a drug mule, is another phenomenon that doesn't reach the eyes and ears of the authorities due to the way these syndicates operate. The boy was found at a taxi rank in the city centre on 9 June. He alleges he was abducted five years ago and has been working as a mule ever since.

Matipa Mwamuka, coordinator of the organisation Activists Networking against the Exploitation of Children (Anex) project against human trafficking, said the boy's case was the first of its kind to be reported to Anex.

'That doesn't mean that similar cases don't exist. One should keep in mind that this is organised crime and the net spans worldwide.'

Anex is currently assisting non-governmental organisations to arrange a place for the boy to stay. They also assist in arranging for a social worker and in attempts to locate the boy's parents.

Captain Frederick van Wyk, police spokesman, said the teenager still has to be interviewed. The inquest could lead to the arrest of members of a drug syndicate.

'The probability of human trafficking will also be investigated.'

Mwamuka said cases of human trafficking where children are lured to South Africa for the commercial sex industry as well as slavery are not often noticed and reported by the public. More awareness is therefore essential. Underaged victims of human trafficking are sometimes, according to her, enticed by other young people and end up in the trap in this way.

'The children are trained by adults to do the work.' Drugs also play a part, particularly with children in the sex industry.

Adult and youthful victims are lured from Zimbabwe, Lesotho and Mozambique.

Mwamuka said sometimes South Africa is the final stop for these victims, but sometimes the country only serves as a passage because of the accessibility of ports and airports.

Locally, human trafficking between provinces is also a problem.

'People are brought to Cape Town from the Northern and Eastern Cape,' Mwamuka said.

Times Live, 6 November 2013

South Africa ranks among the 10 countries in Africa where human trafficking is worst, with 100 000 people reportedly being trafficked in the country annually. And experts believe this number is not a true reflection of the crime as legislative shortcomings hinder prosecutions.

A newly released database shows that the main driving factors for human trafficking in South Africa are sexual exploitation, forced labour, drugs and an alarming new trend of parents selling their children for adoption or sex. Organ trafficking is a growing concern.

The first LexisNexis Human Trafficking Awareness Index – released in Johannesburg yesterday – paints a picture of growing trafficking numbers and a shortage of specialised task teams to investigate the crimes.

Dr Monique Emser, of the KwaZulu-Natal Human Trafficking, Prostitution, Pornography and Brothel Task Team, said: 'South Africans need to be worried. Human trafficking is the final stage in exploitation.

'South Africa is an extremely exploitative society, with poor attitudes regarding women and children. [There is] a low value of life that leads to people being viewed as commodities.'

The database shows that 540 people – 67 of them children – were potentially trafficked into and within South Africa in the last two years, 96 for sexual exploitation, 271 for forced labour, 90 for organ trafficking, four for forced marriages (*unuthwala*) and two as drug mules. Emser said the biggest problem facing South Africa was the lack of a centralised database, even at provincial level. Different government departments and non-governmental organisations have different reporting structures with different classification systems.

Compiled over the past 24 months and to be published

quarterly, the LexisNexis database maps trends, incidents, legal developments and victim and offender profiles. It is the first such report in South Africa. The database was released as the government pushes to establish specialised provincial task teams to respond to trafficking. There are only six such teams currently.

Advocate Thoko Majokweni, head of the sexual offences and community affairs unit at the National Prosecuting Authority, said: 'The biggest [challenge] is legislating correctly. [New legislation] will go a long way to help us monitor and respond correctly to ensure the criminalisation of all forms of human trafficking.'

In February last year – in one of the country's largest anti-trafficking raids – 16 underage girls were rescued from a Durban brothel. In April last year, 200 Cambodian men and boys, who were trafficked to Cape Town for forced labour, were rescued from a fishing vessel.

Billy Last, the LexisNexis South Africa CEO, said the index aimed to show that trafficking was not something that happened only to a few people in faraway countries.

'It is happening right here in South Africa, in our back yards. It is important that as citizens we become more aware of it.'

Despite significant strides in the proclamation of anti-trafficking legislation this year, South Africa lags far behind other countries. A US State Department trafficking report found that, though the South African government was making significant efforts, it did not fully comply with the minimum standards to eliminate trafficking.

'Government departments took preparatory steps, such as developing regulations and policy directives, to be ready to implement the legislation upon enactment . . . however, challenges remain in the identification and investigation of trafficking cases,' it said.

Daily Voice, and iol news, 31 January 2012
South Africa is a hotbed for the billion-dollar human trafficking industry. Even worse, experts say parents often play a role in the modern-day slavery of their own babies and children. People are sold for muti and organ 'donation', babies and children are used for sexual exploitation, cheap labour and even forced marriage.

In Durban, police have found girls as young as 12 years old selling their young bodies on the streets.

The Centre for International Policy's Global Financial Integrity programme estimated last year that global human trafficking accounted for R230 million of illicit trade, only one third behind drugs and counterfeit goods.

In 2000, social workers and officers of the Child Protection Unit estimated there were 28 000 child prostitutes in South Africa.

Joan van Niekerk from Childline says they are still trying to assess exactly how many people have been caught in the human trade.

'However, it is a significant problem in South and Southern Africa and is fed by our high levels of poverty, orphanhood and parental irresponsibility,' she says.

According to Barbara Ras, founder of the Atlantis Women's Movement and a shelter for trafficked victims in Atlantis, there has been an increase in numbers.

'In 2009, we had 16 trafficking victims, in 2010, 35, and last year we had 67,' she tells the *Daily Voice*.

'I think the reason for this spike is that no one is making a noise about it, our courts are too quiet.'

Recently a Joburg teenager told of how she escaped a child trafficking ring. The 16-year-old girl was kidnapped in Bramley last year by four men. After being drugged, she was taken to Khayelitsha where she was raped, beaten, threatened and told she would be put to work as a prostitute. After two months, she managed to escape and was reunited with her family. The Hawks are currently investigating the case.

Barbara says traffickers especially target women and children from rural areas, and often lure them away under the pretext of jobs in the big city.

'These people are poor, there are no jobs, some parents are alcoholics and don't take care of their children,' says Barbara. 'These are innocent girls who go away to work because they think they can get a better life and escape the poverty cycle.'

She says trafficking rings are more sophisticated than people think.

'There's a whole network of people involved – recruiters, taxi drivers, the person waiting in the city, etc. There are even women that help with the trafficking of children and other women,' she explains.

'However, girls are also taken from malls, bus stops and taxi ranks.'

Barbara says traffickers treat the girls well in order to gain their trust.

'The girls are drugged – it's placed in their food and drinks – so by the time they realise they are in trouble, it is far too late,' she says.

'While they are drugged, they are raped and photos are taken of them, which are used to blackmail them. Their clothes and shoes are taken away, so that they don't escape. Some of these girls don't even have breasts yet. They are brought into Cape Town and dropped off in places like Athlone and Goodwood for domestic work where they are treated like slaves.'

Barbara adds: 'In other cases, they are taken to clubs and brothels where they are kept drugged, beaten and abused. They are kept prisoner and are constantly watched. Some girls are even sold from person to person – this problem is bigger than we realise and this came to light through the active work of the city's Vice Squad.'

Barbara says trafficking is done by both local and foreign perpetrators.

'One of the biggest contributing factors to trafficking is that there is too much free access to our borders,' she says. 'We need more border control and national government must make sure we get our specialised units back – we really need them.'

Meanwhile, organisations have called on Parliament to finalise the Prevention and Combating of Trafficking in Persons Bill, also known as the TIP Bill. Currently offenders are charged with sexual abuse, rape and kidnapping.

According to [childrens' rights NGO] Molo Songololo, a large number of cases get dismissed in court due to lack of evidence, poor investigations, poor cooperation from witnesses (victims), and the length of the prosecution process.

'Another danger is when these perpetrators are arrested but not convicted, they come back and search for these girls because they know too much,' adds Barbara. 'The scars never heal for these children, many are so damaged that they go back to the streets and prostitute themselves.

Traffickers are unscrupulous people and they must be brought to book. And if people know about it, they must speak out.'

Let's talk

A second chance

Thank you to Jesus. Wow! He picked me up when I was down in the mud. When I thought death was with me He reached out His hand and lifted me up. Thank you, Jesus, that You love me sincerely and therefore gave me a second chance. Thank you for the times that we laughed and cried together, thank you for the strong hand and arms that have picked me up so many times. Thank you for Your encouraging love, Your warm Father-eyes that can see into my soul. Thank you, Jesus, for a healthy body today, thank you for the times when I could chat with you at night. Thank you that You were there and listened. Thank you, Jesus, for all the times You picked me up when my body and bones were too sick to get up on their own.

Therefore I say today: Thank you, Jesus, for this second chance. I love You so much, Jesus.

Amen

*   *   *

People often ask me, after public appearances, radio talks or motivational events, how I have managed so easily to leave behind all that happened to me in the past. Then I say: no, you are mistaken – it isn't easy. My entire life, from early childhood, was one struggle for survival after another. From a very young age I knew only problems, poverty and struggle. I always thought that perhaps I shouldn't have been born at all. It took me many years to get over everything, but I got a second chance to be able to tell my story today and offer a hand to all the other victims. We will never give up this struggle because every day Jesus gives us the power to fight evil.

To every victim out there – every person who is caught up and whose body is being sold off – know that every day I pray for you. I pray that you will receive the strength and courage to hold on until you are saved. We are trying our best to reach you and to come and get you, because we love you. Therefore we are fighting this evil without fail for you and your freedom. Like soldiers who are ready for battle, we get up every morning and write your names in the sand until we find you. There is hope; hold on to God and your faith until Jesus and his thousands of angels unshackle you and you have your freedom. Because every victim deserves a second chance.

Does God really exist?

'I wish I could see through your eyes, my friend, I wish I could take your pain and make it mine, but all I can do is to hand it to Jesus. He will know what to do with it.'

I often speak with people who tell me about their troubled and terrible childhoods. They always want to know: is there really a God? Because if there is a God, why did He allow all of that to happen to me?

Surely we can't blame God for our parents' and other people's decisions and ways of life? Equally so, I can't blame God when I make certain decisions out of my own free will. God gives us the right and the knowledge to decide for ourselves, but, if I have made the wrong decision, I can't turn around and blame

God at a later stage if my decisions have negative consequences. Similarly, we can't blame God for the way we grew up.

When was the last time you read Psalm 139? And when you read it, did you understand what David is trying to tell us? It took me years to grasp this completely. We humans are tiny in this cruel world we live in, but as tiny as we are, so God is big. Although I rejected God in my younger days so many times, it was still He who carried me through every crisis. Maybe you are going through an intense low in your life at the moment, maybe you don't understand what is happening to you, but there is one thing I learned: always cling to God. When we really grasp how much God loves us, we can pass all our pain and worries to Him. We don't have to carry it ourselves – He will. That is why I have adapted Psalm 139 for myself:

> You surround me from all sides Lord, You see through me. You know me – whether I sit down or whether I get up, You know about it.
>
> You know my thoughts even before I have them. Whether I travel or whether I stay over, You determine that. You are familiar with all my paths. There isn't a word formulated on my tongue, Lord, You don't know what it will be.
>
> You surround me from all sides, You take control of me. The thought overpowers me, it is too great for me to comprehend.
>
> Where would I go to escape Your Spirit? Where would I flee to escape Your presence?
>
> If I climb up to heaven, You are there. When I lie down in the valley of death, You are there also.
>
> If I fly east, or go live in the far west, there also Your hand leads me, Your right hand holds me.
>
> I could ask the darkness to hide me, or the light around

me to turn into night, but for You even the darkness isn't dark, and the night as light as day, darkness as good as light.

Your have shaped me, woven me, in the lap of my mother.

I want to praise You, because You created me in a wondrous way. What You did fills me with wonder. That I know for sure: no bone of mine was hidden from You when I was shaped, where nobody could see it, when I was woven deep in my mother's womb.

You saw me even when I was unborn, all of my days were written down in Your book before my birth. How wonderful Your thoughts are for me, Oh God. How powerful they all are! If I tried to name them all – they are far more than there is sand – and if I was done I would still be involved with You.

Search me, Oh God!

Fathom my heart, examine me, see my restlessness. Determine that I am not on the wrong path, and lead me onto the trusted path!

(Own adaptation of Psalm 139, from
the *New Living Translation* of the Bible)

The day this Psalm makes an impression on your life, you can't but believe that there is a God. You can't but perceive that your Maker knows you this well. Isn't that incredibly wonderful? I wish I had known this Psalm as a child. It would have given me the strength for every day that was filled with loneliness, pain and rejection. But instead of looking for the answers in God's Word, I ran away. We all tend to think our problems will disappear when we run away. It is probably natural to think that way instinctively when things get too much, but it certainly isn't a solution. More so, it doesn't bring healing.

To improve our lives and finally have healing is a process that starts within ourselves. We have to make a conscious decision first before change will be noticeable in our lives. It is pointless to blame others for your circumstances; it won't be of any use to rely on other people to help you and provide direction in your life. No, the only route indicator we have to follow is straight up. Rely on God; trust Him. That is the greatest gift you can ever give yourself.

It also doesn't help to try and escape the scars left by your circumstances and your past. When you deny those scars you will never be able to go through the mourning period on the way to your healing. Take the wounds and give them to God – just like that. Believe me, He wants to take them from you – but you also have to do your bit. If today you are caught up in bad circumstances, or hang out in places that only bring negative energy into your life, you have to make the decision first to break away. Let's look at drug abuse as an example. No matter how you try and justify it, drugs are bad for you. Drug abuse affects your health, inhibits your brain's development and destroys your short-term memory. But this is minor compared to other possible problems. Depending on what drugs you are addicted to and how much you use, it can ruin you financially. You could even lose your job. After that, you can't blame God for your circumstances; it was your own decision. You also can't ask Him every morning to carry the scars from the night before, but tonight you have another pill, snort another line or pour another drink.

Yes, there is a God. He will always give you a second chance. Just ask Him. He will help you to make the right decisions. Just do it.

Alcohol isn't always that innocent

The use of alcohol is a socially acceptable practice, and I am not saying it is wrong. It is, after all, a medical and scientific fact that a glass of wine can be good for your health. The problem isn't the use of alcohol, but its abuse. Let's take a chocolate bar as an example: one bar a week can supplement the required sugar levels in your body, but if you consume three to five bars every day you will develop problems very quickly, especially if you were drinking it down with a litre or more of a soft drink. Before you know it you will be sitting in your doctor's waiting room. That's why I say again: the problem is not so much the use of something, but the abuse. Exactly the same goes for alcohol. It was the same for me and my parents: alcohol was my escape and their idol.

I know my parents did their best for us in their particular way. In spite of all the swearing, poverty and violence, I still don't see my mother as a bad person. I remember her big, beautiful brown eyes, her wide, pretty smile and her softness as a human being that came shining through on occasion. I remember the wonderful times when my mother was sober, how she would hug me and tell me how much she loved me. This pretty picture could have lasted so much longer and might have been so much prettier if alcohol hadn't taken over my parents' lives. They couldn't live without it; without it they couldn't endure their daily pain.

It was their choice to get drunk every night, so they could forget about their scars. There was, however, an alternative they never grabbed hold of: to turn to God and say, 'Dear Lord, I want to escape this vicious cycle. Help me. Take my scars, take my pain, because I can't carry it any more.'

Abuse leaves scars

'Take heaven as your port, the Bible as your map and the
Lord as your guide. That is my best advice.'

After my mother's shooting death, I was admitted to a clinic
where I received treatment for depression. All the patients there
had sad stories. Most of them suffered from suicidal tendencies.
All of them had at some or other stage experienced an ugly crisis
they couldn't cope with. There were young children who had
been molested or raped – young children whose lives hung by
a thread. Every one of these creatures was beautiful and unique
in God's eyes, but to live wasn't an option any more. For a lot
of them, death was the only alternative.

You see, when you have to go through something as inhu-
man as abuse, sexual abuse or rape, a part of your humanity
is taken from you. That person only you knew intimately suddenly doesn't exist. Overnight you lose the inner strength to
stand up against what is wrong and the will to fight against it.
Many of the victims I have worked with changed overnight into
marionettes without a will, being controlled and manipulated
by others. Over time, some of these victims become shadows of
their former selves.

I will never forget the words of Jesus when He said to His
disciples that the children were his:

'Don't keep them from coming to Me, because the kingdom
of the heavens is precisely for people like them.'

(Matthew 19)

Are you also a victim of any form of abuse? Do you feel guilty
that it happened? As victims of sexual abuse, we tend to think

196

it was our fault because we didn't stop it from happening. I understand how you feel, because I had to work through the same emotions. Years ago, when I was still in primary school, time after time I would go with my brother to the teacher's smallholding. I knew what was going to happen, yet I still went there. For an entire year. Why? I don't know. Was I forced, or did I think that maybe it was my duty to submit in exchange for the vegetables and food he gave our family? I don't know. What I do know is that primary school children only want to play. Concepts like blackmail and manipulation are not part of their frame of reference. Afterwards the feelings of guilt would come: why did I allow it? What will people think of me if they find out about it? Am I a sinner and a bad person with no right to exist?

Today I want to say to all the bullies: God sees what you do to others. Even if you suffer your own pain from something that happened in your past, it doesn't give you the right to take it out on others. If you were to look into a mirror, what would you see? Are you proud of what you did? Did it make you a better person? Is it a good feeling to be kicking someone who is already on the ground? Have you ever considered what it must be like being in your victim's shoes? No, because you don't see their tears at night, when everything is quiet, dark and alone. You don't see the why's and the what-for's going through their minds.

My message to you, dear bully, is that God loves you too. He cares about you and He wants to let you have a future too. Stick your hand out and He will take it.

Open up and talk

'Share your hurt and pain with someone and let it all out. When we share our pain with others, tiny windows open to our soul that cleanse and heal everything. Open your window today. Look, Jesus is there, waiting.'

Do you talk about it, or are you too shy because you still feel dirty and humiliated over what happened to you? You wrestle with all these thoughts that bring you down, but you are too scared to open up to someone that you can trust and to talk about it. We, the victims, think if we ignore it all those unpleasant memories will go away. Let's rather bury it far away and hope that it will somehow vanish. Yes, to pack it away will probably suppress the pain for a while, but in this way you will never find healing.

No, my dear friend, it will not go away. It won't help if you keep all those negative emotions bottled up inside you. It has to be released. You have to talk to someone about it, because the first step to healing is to open up that raw wound inside you. You can do it. And when you do it, I promise you, you will feel like a new person. Take the first step today and talk to Jesus about what has happened to you. He is waiting on you to share your pain with Him and that you will trust Him with all of it. When you do that the old wound drops from your body and the light of Jesus shines through. Like a carpenter, He comes to plane and work on you so as to reshape you into the person you once were.

Forgiveness or hate?

We can't always choose what happens to us, but we can choose what we're going to do with it. Are you going to bear a grudge? Are you going to pamper the hate for the person who did it to you? You can, but then you will eventually become a bitter person with pain in your heart. That pain will grow larger and larger. Or will you forgive, pick up the pieces of your life and create a new path for yourself? The choice is yours.

Hatefulness is an extremely negative emotion that can take over our hearts so completely that there isn't space left over even for God to do His work. Often we complain that God's light, His healing hand, isn't visible in our lives, but often it is just because we don't allow Him the necessary space for it.

Initially, I walked the destructive path of hate and condemnation. The grudge I carried inside me eventually dominated my life to such an extent that I couldn't focus on the future and on everything that really mattered. Every day I thought about what had happened to me. I pampered every moment of humiliation and getting hurt until one day I visited my pastor again. I was inside a prison, a prison of my own decisions, and I blamed God all the time for what had happened to me. I was angry and asked God to let something terrible happen to all of those people who had hurt me. I was looking for revenge, but He didn't take it. He had a different, better and greater plan. Forgiveness. I could hear His voice clearly inside me: You have to forgive first before your pain can be healed; you must forgive first before positive things can be released into your life; you must forgive first so I can have the space to do wonders in your life.

I suddenly saw the bigger picture. I saw Jesus on the cross praying for His assailants: 'God, forgive them, because they don't know what they are doing.'

I started crying. Suddenly I wasn't the adult, vengeful woman any more, but the little girl in search of love, acceptance and nurturing. And security. I got down on my knees and just started talking to Jesus:

'Dear Jesus, this morning I bow at your feet and bring my pain to You, because, dear Lord, I don't know what to do with it. It eats away at me like cancer, I am lost and carry so much pain in my heart. Dear Jesus, You are my Creator and my Maker. Only You know me infinitely well and only You, my Jesus, know my brokenness and pain. This morning I come to you because I want to be free. Therefore I forgive every person who ever did me harm.

I forgive my parents for the desperate circumstances I grew up in. I forgive them for every night I had to go to bed on an empty stomach, for every bit of verbal abuse, for every time they were intoxicated and I was exposed to their violence. I forgive the teacher who touched me inappropriately when I was a little primary school girl and who did things to me he shouldn't have. I forgive the person who took me to the club and sold me. I forgive the club owners for everything I had to endure there against my will. I forgive every man who rented my body during that time, who humiliated me, who assaulted me. I forgive them all.

Today I ask that You will also forgive all of them. I don't know their life stories or backgrounds; I don't know why they did those things to me and therefore I cannot judge them.

Dear Jesus, this weak body of mine belongs to You only, but it is broken. That is why I bring it to You for healing. Wash my body with Your blood so that I can be clean and that my future path will be a hospital for other victims like me, so that I can help them. I know, my Lord, that You are my Shepherd and my God and that no person on this earth will harm me ever again.

Thank you, Jesus, that You died on the cross for my sins, and for the sins of every person who harmed me.

Amen'

After I had forgiven everyone I opened rooms in my life for God that He filled with treasures. But I didn't only open doors for Him; He opened doors for me as well.

A loved one's death shatters

'Jesus, I don't understand everything. I have so many questions I need answers for, but right now I just want to come and sit at your feet with my pain and cry. I just want to feel your arms around me. Because I know that by being in Your presence I will feel better.'

Every day we continue with our lives as if tomorrow is a given. In the mornings or at night we greet our family members casually as if we will naturally see them again later. But life isn't really that predictable. Have you ever considered the possibility that when you come home tonight your partner, your parents or maybe your child may not be with you any more? Have you ever considered that maybe tomorrow your loved one won't be in your life any more? The mere thought is unsettling. Today we are here and tomorrow we're gone.

Losing a loved one unexpectedly is probably one of the most traumatic experiences a person can have. Afterwards you experience a muddle of emotions and different phases. Are you in such a phase of your life? Believe me, dear friend, I know how you feel. My brother passed away recently, before him my father and, when I was still at school, my mother. One of the first emotions is denial and disbelief. No, it can't be true! How could it happen? It just cannot be! Then comes the anger. And often this anger is directed at God. That morning in 1993 (I was in standard eight) when I discovered my dead mother in her bedroom. I was angry at God for a very long time. I blamed Him for her shooting death because He had allowed it to happen. Initially I shouted at Him, but later started wondering whether there really was a God. When I think of that now, I realise that with such an attitude you close your ears to the words and encouragement of others close to you. They can sympathise, they can offer help, they can pray for you – but you are totally deaf to all of that.

After my mother's death I received a lot of counselling in the clinic to which I was admitted, but later from many pastoral leaders as well. One of the concepts I will never forget is that of acceptance. Only when you accept death can the road to healing begin. You have to realise, and accept, that the person is dead. But what does acceptance of death mean? The question milled through my young mind way back in those days. Acceptance is such a big word. Way too big for a child – and sometimes for adults as well – to comprehend. What is it? How does one accept death? Is it like breaking up with your boyfriend? Or is it like accepting the fact that you are not good at mathematics? Did I simply have to accept that it was her time to die? All these things went through my head, and nothing made any sense. I didn't want to talk to anyone, not even to God, because I was still too angry at Him. Later, when I was in the club, I got even angrier at Him. But mercifully, in spite of everything, God never keeps His love from us.

Only three years after my mother's death did I have the confidence to return to God. I didn't know what to say to him; I simply asked Him if I could sit at His feet. I didn't want to say anything, I didn't want to cry. I just wanted to be with Him. Suddenly the most amazing feeling came over me. Serenity, acceptance, contentment. And I knew the God I rejected for so long had never deserted me.

Don't look down on others

I hated suicide for years following my mother's death. I thought it was the biggest sin ever, and I would say that anyone who committed suicide was weak and didn't have strength of character. Once again God brought me to my knees, and He wanted to know why I was judging something like that, when only He could judge. Who gave me the right to exert my opinion so brutally? At that stage of my life I was very vengeful. I would give people a piece of my mind, I thought I was a better person and that the world owed me something. And this is how I stepped into the trap of superiority. A place from where one condemns others. I despised not only people with suicidal thoughts but also tramps, beggars, the rich, as well as prostitutes. I was so angry at life that I actually hated everything and everyone around me.

Aren't you perhaps in a similar place today? When driving to work this morning, in what way did you look at the beggar at the traffic lights? Did you look down upon him and think you were so much better than him, because at least you have a house, a car or a job? Yes, I was in such a place for a very long time. To me, beggars were the scum of the earth, people who were too lazy to go looking for a job. Until the Lord once again brought me to my senses and reminded me where I came from. As a child, I had to beg or steal to stay alive. When my mother was sober she would bake banana bread or make home decorations that I had to go and sell door to door in our neighbourhood. I did it, because when people find themselves in such a situation they do anything to survive. When I see children begging these days I remind myself of what my life was like in those days. To stare people in the face all day for money is very destructive; it belittles you and harms your humanity.

Before looking down on a beggar again, stop and talk to him, because you don't know his circumstances. Look at his sunburnt skin, dry lips and tattered clothes. Become part of his life and stand in his shoes for just a moment. Maybe then you will have greater compassion for him. And when you hand him something, be thankful that God has blessed you with the financial means to help others.

If you can't stand in another person's shoes, then you can't throw stones . . .

Advice for teenagers

'I don't want to be staying with my mum and dad any more. I don't like it there. I think I am going to run away.'

I often receive messages like this, whether an SMS or WhatsApp or through Facebook, from children I meet during my talks at schools. The underlying message is always the same: their circumstances at home have become unbearable. Now all they want to do is run away. To where they don't know – just as long as they can get away. To a better life, they often believe. To them I say: my dear teenager, I know how you feel, and I don't judge you at all. But today I can tell you it's not the best solution to your problems. Remember, I felt exactly the same. When I was a teenager I also wanted with all my might to run away from home. And after I ran away I ended up at the club, where I was kept a prisoner. Then I would have done anything just to be reunited with my family again. Running away from home is definitely not the solution, because you don't know what's awaiting you in the unknown. For me that was hell itself. Rather talk to someone you can trust and who can help you. A spiritual adviser, a teacher, a social worker, a family

204

member. There are also many Christian counselling groups on Facebook where you can pour out your heart. There really are many people who would like to, and will, offer help. Just ask.

Help yourself in these ways:

- Avoid drugs at all costs; they only bring tears. You can so easily destroy a wonderful future by trying to be one of the crowd. So many addicted teenagers I have talked to have told me they simply wanted to try it just that one time. Drugs aren't something you can try only once – that one time can very easily spell the beginning of the end for you. Mercifully, I was saved from a death from drugs, but overcoming my addiction was absolute hell.
- Avoid intimate contact with strangers. Don't start unnecessary conversations, drive somewhere with a stranger or hand out your contact details or home address just like that. Say 'no, thanks' when a stranger offers you something to drink, even if it's at a get-together with your friends. Be very careful whom you talk to on social platforms like Mxit, Twitter, BBM and WhatsApp. Don't ever accept an invitation from someone you don't know.
- Don't believe everything you hear. Do proper research first before you make a decision or become involved with something, especially if someone offers you work or a part-time income. All the so-called get-rich-quick schemes are a farce – avoid them. There is only one way to earn money and that is to work for it. Do you know how many South African girls are currently locked up in foreign jails because they believed local drug dealers' stories that 'you can make lots of money by simply collecting a parcel from an overseas friend of mine'? Or how many girls have been raped –

or murdered – after responding to an anonymous advertisement that promised them 'thousands of rands and fame' in the world of modelling? If something appears too good to be true, it usually is. Be extra-careful: even if an advertisement or job offer appears plausible, always let your parents go with you to the interview or audition.

- Establish a relationship with your parents that is based on mutual trust. Discuss the latest fashion crazes and trends in the teenage world with them. Never lie to them about where you are going or what you are doing. Other teenagers might think it uncool to have an honest relationship with their parents, but it will make a winner out of you, not a victim. Appreciate your parents; believe me, teenagers never fully comprehend what their parents have had to endure in order to raise them. Parents also make mistakes, but don't condemn them for it, just like you wouldn't want them to condemn you for your mistakes. Try to understand your parents' situation, exactly the way you would like them to understand yours.

- No parent can always give their children everything they want – accept and understand that. Also, never compare your parents to your friends' parents. Remember, they do for you what their circumstances allow them to do. Appreciate your parents; you will never be able to replace them. A quick SMS message thanking them for what they do for you will do them the world of good. Don't let the fast-paced world we live in drive a wedge between you and your parents. If there is a problem, talk to them or write them a note. How are they supposed to know what's happening with you when you don't communicate with them? Appreciate the space they give you and never abuse it.

- If you are at a party and something doesn't feel right, contact your parents immediately so that they can come and fetch you. You might get to know one side of a friend at school, but another, darker side might appear when you are out together somewhere. If you are forced to do something you know isn't right, or you end up in some kind of uncomfortable situation, call somebody immediately to come and fetch you. When you go out, check that your cellphone is fully charged and keep it close to you all the time. Ensure that all possible emergency numbers are stored on your phone.

- Keep your body, deeds, thoughts and words clean and pure the way God meant for you. You are too precious to waste what you have been given. Dear young girl: provocative clothing like miniskirts won't help you find a proper boyfriend. And dear boy: swearing, smoking, drinking and other irresponsible behaviour won't draw the right attention. Money, the latest fashion crazes or designer clothes won't make you a better person. It is what's on the inside – your soul, your personality and your nature – that will shape you into a beautiful person. I also don't think it's a very good idea to be hanging out in clubs while you are still at school. There is too much evil that you, as a child, are ill-equipped to deal with. Wait until you are an adult before you start doing adult things.

- You only have one life and that life is precious to your friends, your family, your parents and God. Your humanity has an impact on everyone around you. Live your life in such a way that everyone can see Jesus in you. The world is cruel and dangerous. Be aware of the danger around you, be careful and know what to do should something happen to you. Don't walk places alone. Always stay in a group, because criminals prefer to target individuals rather than groups of people. Avoid all forms of Satanism – it isn't as cool as you might think. Believe me, I know!

Advice for parents

'Sometimes we as parents make mistakes we don't want our children to notice. Even if we are not perfect we can still try to create a safe environment for our children. That is the foundation you lay for them, after all.'

The only reason I tell my story is to share the lessons I have learnt. Every child's life I can save in this way, every relationship between a teenager and his parents I can mend, makes all my experiences worthwhile. But every story I hear tugs at my heart. Like the mother who called me in August 2012 after I did an interview on RSG: her child had run away from home and disappeared. She wished she had a better relationship with her child and knew what was going on in her life, she told me sadly.

Yes, many cases of children reported missing are often children who have run away from home. If by any chance you have a broken relationship with your children, do whatever it takes to make it right, even if it means getting professional help. Make time for your children and sit down and chat with them. Discover how they feel about things and how they see life, even if you disagree with them and what they say hurts you. Our families are little gifts God gives us to take care of Him. Nurture each other. Don't let anger, pain and unforgiving come between you and the people close to you. Teenagers get confused and they get hurt. On top of that, the pressure teenagers experience these days on a social level is far more intense than years ago when we were children ourselves. Give your children the space to find themselves within the framework of your wisdom and insight.

Know your children. That really is the most important piece

of advice I can offer parents. Know who they are, what they are thinking, what their dreams and fears are, who their friends are. Know what is happening on their computers, what they google and on which social platforms they are active. And the only way you can achieve this is by making time for them, talking to them and sharing precious moments with them. Work on a relationship where mutual respect is key, where you are your children's best friend and where they have the confidence to come to you with any issue, worry or problem.

Help your children in these ways:

- Don't let your children walk to school alone. If you can't drop them off or pick them up every day, join lift clubs. Children from the same neighbourhood can also walk together, as attackers usually target individuals. The same goes for visits to the movies or shopping malls.
- Know where your children are at all times, who they are visiting and what they are doing. Lay down strict rules about what time they have to be home again or what time you will pick them up.
- Ensure your children's school doesn't allow the learners to leave the school grounds during break time. I know of a number of cases where a child has slipped out to the café across the street, only to be picked up by an attacker.
- Be involved when your children apply for part-time work or holiday jobs. Go along to the interview and ensure the employer and the business are above suspicion. The wording of the advertisement may sound innocent, but your children could very easily become trapped in a sex and drug network. Be particularly wary of advertisements looking for girls to become hostesses.

- If you suspect your child is using drugs, get help immediately. Drug abusers are easy targets for syndicates recruiting teenagers to sell drugs for pocket money.
- Money and an abundance of luxury items aren't substitutes for an uninvolved parent. Money also can't buy love and respect.
- Today, modern technology offers a variety of tracking possibilities, like software that can be uploaded onto a cellphone to monitor the user's movements. The People Search and Rescue Unit also offers such a service. It might be a good idea to use this as a precautionary measure, but discuss it with your children first so they will understand why you're doing it and that it will be in their own interests. If you suspect your child is missing, act immediately. The first hour is vitally important. As a parent, you need to know immediately what to do, who to call and where to go. I provide my e-mail address with the greatest of pleasure should you have any questions: stoptrafficking@live.com. For more advice, visit the following web pages:

  Missing Children South Africa: www.missingchildrensa.org.za

  People Search and Rescue Unit: www.PSARU.co.za

  The Salvation Army Southern Africa Territory: www.salvationarmy.org.za

  The A21 Campaign South Africa: www.thea21campaign.org

Conclusion

Would I have wanted my life – as a toddler, teenager, and adult up to where I am today – to have been different in any way? That is a very difficult question. I was a broken person after what happened to me in Bloemfontein as a teenage sex slave.

But God's grace and love healed me through the years. I went through all the pain, humiliation and struggle for a purpose: to become a warrior for God and to work for Him on this earth.

My purpose is to bring Home all His children – the lost and the victims. I won't be able to save all of them, as much as I would like to. Some days I become furious when I witness what is happening to our teenagers; some days I feel desperate and powerless against the onslaught of evil. Some days I know the road ahead won't be an easy one. But then I experience God's power again, time after time. I experience how He strengthens me, how He uses me, and how He gives me His power and love to carry through what we do. We are not afraid of the sex syndicates and the gang leaders because God sends His angels to protect us.

For those making money from the bodies of innocent victims, I have the following message: we won't give up and you won't get the better of us. We will come and save the victims, one after the other. We will dig and scratch until we know where you are keeping them. We will come, without fear, because we are surrounded by the angels of our Maker, Father and God.

Acknowledgements

To my daughter, Michaela Davis, for her patience, for always accepting everything and for standing by me. Thank you, Miekie, for your love and for the person you are today. With your beautiful love and heart for others, you are an inspiration to me. I live only for you and for all the people out there experiencing pain. You, my child, are absolutely exceptional!

My sister, you were my mother, my friend, my dad, just about everything. The times when I was locked away in the cupboards, you brought me bread and water secretly. You had to take on the motherly duties when you were a child yourself. My older sister, we often discuss our childhood when we're together, but today I just want to say thank you. It's such a small word, but thanks, Ronel, thanks for what you did for me. This book is dedicated to you. Just know that I love you very much. I am also incredibly proud of you because you quit drinking in August 2013. I don't have words . . . thank you, my sister.

Thank you, Johan Kruger, for your devotion, unending patience and love. Those times when I got so very lost, you took my hand and got me back on the road. Thank you for always believing in me – even when the world got too much for me. Thank you for your shoulder and calls, SMSs and messages. Thank you for what you mean to Miekie, that you took over the fatherly duties and brought her up so beautifully. Thank you so much for who and what you are today.

Thank you, Hykie Berg, you are awesome . . . you have gone through so much that people know so little about, and look at you today! You have a heart of gold. I have been filled with so much hope with everything you have achieved in your life, and often it was your SMSs or encouragement that gave me the strength to carry on.

Thank you also, Nico Panagio, for your wonderful passion for the people out there. Thank you for fighting heart and soul for every missing person.

My biggest thanks to Jaco Hough-Coetzee, who adapted the manuscript. The day I met you, I just wanted to sit around with a glass of wine, but we focused on the book. Still, we were like two old friends who could just chat. The times you called, I could sense this book meant a lot to you. You put your heart and soul into it, you sweated blood and I allowed you into a world drenched in pain. I shared things with you that were very personal – deep, hurtful things – but you never thought poorly of me. Thank you that I could trust you with my pain, thank you for taking over and putting your trust in me; you are a star.

Then to the dearest Ingeborg Pelser: if it wasn't for you, your faith and trust, this book would not have seen the light of day. Thank you for your compassion, your positive attitude, your friendliness and your faith. Your perseverance and guidance taught me a lot. You worked so hard on this and never gave up. Thank you very, very much.

And finally, but first really, my Maker, my Saviour. Jesus, You took me from the gutter and healed me. When I was at my weakest and caved in completely, You took me in Your arms. You taught me about forgiving; I had to forgive, otherwise I would still be caught up in a prison of unforgiving and I wouldn't be free. When You woke me in the middle of the night for the first time, I knew You were my only and true hope. You talked to me, You picked up my pieces that were scattered everywhere and put them together again with Your love. I always wondered why I am on this earth and why somebody like You could love me, but You taught me also to tell others about You and thus be redeemed from the hurt and pain. Father, today I ask for strength and even more strength to tackle everything that still lies ahead. Without You it is impossible. Thank you, Jesus, for everything You have done for me, thank you, Lord, that You are in my life.

www.ingramcontent.com/pod-product-compliance
Lightning Source LLC
Chambersburg PA
CBHW062054270326

41931CB00013B/3063